DESSERTS

OVER 150 DELICIOUS IDEAS

DESSERTS

OVER 150 DELICIOUS IDEAS

a Salamander book

Published by Salamander Books Limited
LONDON • NEW YORK

Published by Salamander Books Ltd.,
129-137 York Way, London N7 9LG, United Kingdom

©Salamander Books Ltd. 1993

Recipes and photographs on the following pages are the copyright
of Merehurst Press, and credited as follows: 26, 34, 35, 36, 37,
38, 39, 40, 41, 42, 43, 44.

ISBN 0 86101 701 3

Distributed by Hodder and Stoughton Services, P.O. Box 6,
Mill Road, Dunton Green, Sevenoaks, Kent TN13 2YG

All correspondence concerning the content of this volume should
be addressed to Salamander Books Ltd.

1 3 5 7 9 8 6 4 2

CREDITS
Contributing authors: Janice Murfitt, Mary Norwak and Sally Taylor
Photographers: David Gill, Paul Grater and Jon Stewart
Typeset by: The Old Mill, London
Colour separation by: Scantrans Pte Ltd, Singapore

Printed in Italy

Contents

Introduction

There can be no doubt about desserts—they are the crowning glory of a meal; the final expression of the thought and care you have taken in preparation and cooking. Whether you serve a homely Bread & Butter Pudding or an exotic Choc Chestnut Gâteau, you can be sure that it will be greeted with delight by all at the table.

There are desserts for everybody and every season in this delicious collection. Such all-time favourites as Queen of Puddings, Pancakes, Oeufs à Neige and Strawberry Milk Jelly will bring a smile to the faces of all children, and many a grown-up too! For an elegant lunch or dinner party, choose from such classics as Crème Brûlée, Charlotte Russe, Dacquoise or Hot Chocolate Soufflé, or delight your guests with something a little more unusual such as Framboise Zabaglione or Grapefruit Cheesecake.

Many of the desserts in this book are extremely economical as well as quick and easy to make, while others, for those special occasions, require a little more time and costly ingredients. You can really let your imagination run riot decorating desserts: many of the quick desserts can be turned into party puddings simply by decorating them with rosettes of whipped cream, crystalized fruits, sugar flowers or edible flowers from the garden. Or lift an everyday pudding into the realms of the special by serving it with one of the delicious sauces from the chapter of sauces and accompaniments.

Points for Perfect Desserts

Remember these few key points when planning a dessert, particularly for a special occasion

● Serve a delicate dessert after a substantial starter and main course; if you wish to serve a hearty sweet course, keep the preceding courses light.

● Consider the textures in the meal and include crisp foods to contrast with soft or creamy dishes. Serve crisp biscuits with smooth desserts.

● Refreshing citrus desserts and ices follow spicy foods well.

● Plan a simple, prepare-ahead dessert if you are concentrating on last-minute dishes for the first part of the meal.

● If you intend serving a spectacular baked soufflé or similar sweet course which requires undivided last-minute attention, then prepare all the ingredients, utensils and cooking containers in advance. Prepare the recipe as far as possible beforehand.

● It is quite usual to offer a choice of desserts for a dinner party. In this case select two quite different dishes, often including one very light dessert as an alternative to a rich confection.

● Lastly, remember to warn guests not to overindulge in the savoury courses if you have a spectacular and filling concoction making an entry at the end of the meal.

CREAMS, CUSTARDS
& DAIRY DESSERTS

CRUNCHY PEACHES

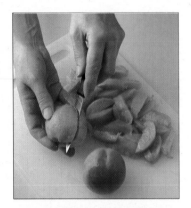

6 peaches
4 tablespoons maraschino or similar cherry liqueur
315 ml (10 fl oz/1¼ cups) whipping cream
60 g (2 oz/⅓ cup) demerara sugar

Blanch peaches in boiling water for 1 minute. Drain and peel off skin. Cut flesh into thick slices. Discard stones.

Place peach slices in a shallow heatproof dish, filling dish evenly. Pour liqueur over slices. In a bowl, whip cream stiffly and place spoonfuls on top of peaches. Gently spread cream evenly. Cover dish with plastic wrap and refrigerate for at least 4 hours.

Just before serving, heat grill to very high. Remove plastic wrap from dish and spoon sugar evenly over top of cream. Place under the grill until sugar has dissolved and caramellized. Serve the peaches immediately.

Serves 6.

Note: Liqueurs are expensive, but there is no point in skimping for this dish – you need to add enough liqueur to make sure the flavour comes through.

PINEAPPLE CREAM

3 slices fresh pineapple
440 g (14 oz) can evaporated milk, well chilled
2 teaspoons powdered gelatine
juice of ½ lemon
caster sugar, to taste

TO DECORATE: crystalized pineapple
crystalized angelica

Cut away all skin and 'eyes' from pineapple and cut out core. Purée the flesh in a blender or food processor.

In a bowl, whip evaporated milk until thick and creamy. Sprinkle gelatine over lemon juice in a small bowl and leave to soften for 2-3 minutes. Stand bowl in a saucepan of hot water and stir until the gelatine has dissolved. Stir it into the whipped milk.

Fold pineapple purée into whipped milk and sweeten to taste with sugar. Pour into a glass serving bowl or individual glasses and chill until set. Decorate with crystalized pineapple and angelica cut into leaf shapes just before serving.

Serves 4.

CRÈME BRÛLÉE

CITRUS FLUMMERY

4 egg yolks
2½ teaspoons caster sugar
pinch of cornflour
625 ml (20 fl oz/2½ cups) whipping cream
2 vanilla pods
frosted flowers, to decorate, if desired

CARAMEL TOPPING: caster sugar

In a large bowl, beat egg yolks lightly with sugar and cornflour.

Put cream into a saucepan. With a sharp knife, split open vanilla pods and scrape seeds into cream. Bring almost to boiling point, then pour onto yolks, beating all the time. Pour into top of a double boiler, or a bowl set over a pan of simmering water, and cook over medium heat until mixture thickens sufficiently to coat the back of spoon. Pour into shallow gratin dish. Leave to cool, then chill in the refrigerator overnight.

Two hours before serving, heat grill to very high. Cover surface of pudding thickly and evenly with sugar and place under grill until the sugar has caramelized. Chill for 2 hours. Decorate with frosted flowers, if desired.

Serves 4-6.

Note: The best vanilla pods are coated in white crystals and are very expensive. All vanilla pods can be washed after use and used again. Store them in a dry place.

75 ml (2½ fl oz/⅓ cup) frozen concentrated orange and
   passion fruit juice
315 ml (10 fl oz/1¼ cups) double (thick) cream
1 egg white
30 g (1 oz/5 teaspoons) caster sugar (see Note)
orange wedges and passion fruit, to decorate
langues de chat biscuits, to serve

Thaw concentrated fruit juice and measure out required quantity. (Use remainder as a drink, making up with water.) In a bowl, whip cream to soft peaks.

Add juice gradually, continuing to whip cream, until fairly thick.

In a separate bowl, whisk egg white until stiff. Whisk in sugar, then fold into creamy mixture. Spoon into individual glasses and chill for 1 hour. Decorate with orange wedges and passion fruit. Serve with the biscuits.

Serves 4-6.

Note: Flavour the sugar for this and other desserts and cakes by keeping it in a jar with a vanilla pod. This will give the sugar a strong vanilla flavour.

TIPSY FRUIT FOOL

FRAMBOISE ZABAGLIONE

500 g (1 lb) cooking apples, peeled and sliced
185 g (6 oz/2¼ cups) pre-soaked dried apricots
60 g (2 oz/¼ cup) caster sugar
pared peel and juice of 3 satsumas
6 teaspoons apricot brandy
90 ml (3 fl oz/⅓ cup) fromage frais
chocolate curls, to decorate, if desired

In a saucepan, place apples, apricots, sugar, satsuma peel and juice. Bring to boil, cover and cook until apples and apricots are tender. Remove satsuma peel, reserve some for decoration. Leave until cold.

Pour cold apple and apricot mixture into a food processor fitted with a metal blade. Process until puréed. Add apricot brandy and fromage frais and process until well blended. Divide mixture between individual glasses and chill until required.

Using a sharp knife, cut reserved satsuma peel into needle shreds or thin strips and use to decorate top of each dessert, adding a few chocolate curls, if desired.

Serves 6.

4 egg yolks
220 ml (7 fl oz/⅞ cup) Framboise liqueur
30 g (1 oz/5 teaspoons) caster sugar
strawberries or raspberries, to decorate, if desired
langues de chat biscuits, to serve

Put egg yolks, liqueur and sugar into a double boiler or a bowl set over a saucepan of simmering water.

Set over a medium heat and, using a balloon whisk, whisk the mixture until it is very thick and mousse-like in appearance – this will take about 20 minutes.

Pour mixture into glasses, decorate with strawberries or raspberries if desired, and serve immediately, while still warm, with langues de chat biscuits.

Serves 4.

Note: Although it is laborious it is important to use a hand whisk for this recipe. An electric whisk increases the volume of the eggs too quickly, so that they do not have a chance to cook. The mixture will then collapse when it is poured into glasses.

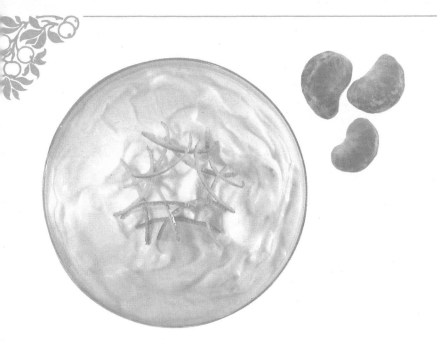

TANGERINE SYLLABUB

grated peel and juice of 3 tangerines
grated peel and juice of 1 lemon
90 g (3 oz/⅓ cup) caster sugar
90 ml (3 fl oz/⅓ cup) cream sherry
315 ml (10 fl oz/1¼ cups) double (thick) cream
extra grated peel, to decorate, if desired

Put tangerine and lemon peel and both juices into a bowl with sugar and sherry and leave to infuse in a cool place for at least 1 hour.

In a large bowl, whip the cream while gradually pouring in the infused mixture. Keep whipping until mixture is thick enough to form soft peaks.

Pour mixture into a glass serving bowl or individual glasses and chill for at least 2 hours before serving. Decorate with extra peel, if desired.

Serves 4-6.

Note: Use a sharp grater to grate the peel of tangerines, otherwise the peel tends to tear. Warm citrus fruits slightly before squeezing and they will yield more juice.

VANILLA BAVAROIS

375 ml (12 fl oz/1½ cups) milk
1 vanilla pod or 3 drops vanilla essence
3 egg yolks
30 g (1 oz/5 teaspoons) caster sugar
3 teaspoons powdered gelatine
pinch of grated nutmeg, if desired
185 ml (6 fl oz/¾ cup) whipping cream
Blackcurrant Sauce (see page 90) or Dark Chocolate Sauce (see page 92), to serve
grated chocolate, to decorate if desired

Put milk and vanilla pod or essence into a saucepan and bring almost to boiling point. Remove from heat.

In a bowl, beat egg yolks and sugar until thick and mousse-like. Pour hot milk onto mixture, beating all the time. Return to saucepan, and stir over low heat until mixture has thickened sufficiently to coat back of spoon. Set aside. Sprinkle gelatine over 5 tablespoons water in a small bowl and leave to soften for 2-3 minutes. Stand bowl in a saucepan of hot water and stir until the gelatine has dissolved. Add to milk mixture, stirring well, then leave to cool, stirring occasionally.

When mixture is on point of setting, add grated nutmeg, if using. Whip cream lightly and fold into mixture. Spoon into a lightly oiled 940 ml (30 fl oz/3¾ cup) mould and refrigerate until set. Turn out and serve with sauce. Decorate with chocolate, if desired.

Serves 4-6.

Variations: Make the bavarois in individual moulds. For Lemon Bavarois, dissolve gelatine in juice of 1 large lemon instead of water and add lemon peel.

ROSE CREAM

625 ml (20 fl oz/2½ cups) whipping cream
3 teaspoons powdered gelatine
5-6 teaspoons triple strength rosewater
grated peel and juice of 1 lemon
60 g (2 oz/¼ cup) caster sugar

ROSE PETALS: 1 egg white
petals from 1 rose
caster sugar

To prepare rose petals, preheat oven to 110C (225F/Gas ¼). Whisk egg white until frothy and dip rose petals in to cover.

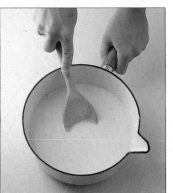

Toss petals in caster sugar and place on baking tray covered with silicone paper. Bake in the bottom of oven for about 2½ hours, leaving oven door slightly ajar, until dry and hard. Place all ingredients for cream in a heavy-based saucepan and stir over a very low heat until gelatine and sugar have dissolved. Do not allow to boil.

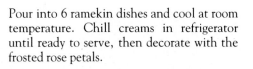

Pour into 6 ramekin dishes and cool at room temperature. Chill creams in refrigerator until ready to serve, then decorate with the frosted rose petals.

Serves 6.

Note: The rose petals can be prepared in advance and stored in an airtight tin. For extra colour, decorate with frosted rose leaves as well as petals but do not eat them.

CREAMY CRANBERRY FOOL

185 g (6 oz) cranberries, fresh or frozen, thawed if frozen
90 ml (3 fl oz/⅓ cup) orange juice
185 g (6 oz/¾ cup) caster sugar
315 ml (10 fl oz/1¼ cups) whipping cream
grated orange peel, to decorate

Put cranberries into a saucepan with orange juice and sugar and simmer for about 10 minutes, until berries pop. Set aside to cool.

When cranberries are cold, rub through a fine metal sieve, using a wooden spoon. In a large bowl, whip cream until stiff and fold in purée. Chill until ready to serve.

Serve fool in individual glasses topped with a little grated orange peel.

Serves 4.

Note: Substitute 250 g (8 oz) damson for the cranberries. Cook them with 3 tablespoons water and omit orange juice.

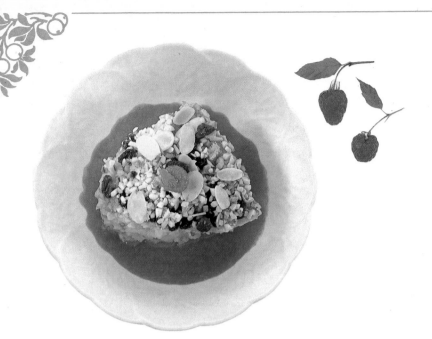

CABINET PUDDING

60 g (2 oz/⅓ cup) raisins
2 tablespoons rum, brandy or water
315 g (10 oz) chocolate or plain sponge cake
125 g (4 oz/½ cup) caster sugar
125 g (4 oz/1 cup) chopped mixed nuts
4 eggs
500 ml (16 fl oz/2 cups) milk
30 g (1 oz/¼ cup) flaked almonds
raspberries, to decorate
Raspberry Sauce (see page 91), to serve

Soak raisins in rum, brandy or water for at least 1 hour. Meanwhile, preheat oven to 180C (350F/Gas 4). Lightly butter a 1.25 litre (40 fl oz/5 cup) pie dish.

Roughly break up sponge cake and put into prepared pie dish. Add raisins and soaking liquid, then sprinkle with just over one-quarter of sugar and all chopped mixed nuts. In a bowl, beat eggs with remaining sugar and whisk in milk. Pour into pie dish. Scatter with flaked almonds.

Put pie dish into a roasting tin and add enough boiling water to come halfway up sides. Bake in the oven for 1-1½ hours, until lightly set. Decorate with raspberries and serve hot with Raspberry Sauce.

Serves 6.

Note: Stale, leftover sponge is ideal for this pudding, or ratafias can be used in place of sponge cake, if preferred.

ALMOND BLANCMANGE

90 g (3 oz/½ cup) whole blanched almonds
4 egg yolks
125 g (4 oz/½ cup) caster sugar
375 ml (12 fl oz/1½ cups) milk
3 teaspoons powdered gelatine
250 ml (8 fl oz/1 cup) whipping cream
toasted flaked almonds and herb sprigs, to decorate

Toast whole blanched almonds, turning frequently to brown evenly. Cool and grind coarsely in a coffee grinder or food processor.

In a bowl, beat egg yolks and sugar until thick and mousse-like. Put milk into a saucepan and bring almost to boiling point. Beat into egg mixture. Return to saucepan, and stir over low heat until mixture has thickened sufficiently to coat the back of the spoon. Do not boil. Remove from heat and leave to cool. Sprinkle gelatine over 3 tablespoons water in a small bowl and leave to soften for 2-3 minutes. Stand bowl in a saucepan of hot water and stir until gelatine has dissolved. Stir into milk mixture.

In another bowl, whip cream lightly. When milk mixture is on point of setting, stir in ground almonds and fold in cream. Spoon into a serving dish or individual glasses and chill until set. When ready to serve, decorate with toasted flaked almonds and herb sprigs.

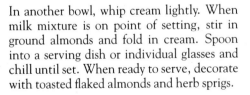

Serves 6.

Note: Grind whole nuts rather than buying them ready ground for the best flavour. Toasting them helps to bring out the flavour still further.

ROSE CUSTARDS

ENGLISH TRIFLE

315 ml (10 fl oz/1¼ cups) milk
315 ml (10 fl oz/1¼ cups) double (thick) cream
2 eggs
2 egg yolks
30 g (1 oz/5 teaspoons) caster sugar
8 teaspoons rose water

MARINATED FRUIT: 4 teaspoons rose water
4 teaspoons rosé wine
8 teaspoons icing sugar
petals from 2 scented roses
125 g (4 oz) strawberries, sliced
125 g (4 oz) raspberries, thawed if frozen
1 star fruit, sliced

1 egg, plus 2 egg yolks
30 g (1 oz/5 teaspoons) caster sugar
315 ml (10 fl oz/1¼ cups) milk
few drops vanilla essence
20 sponge fingers
6 teaspoons Madeira
3 teaspoons brandy
6 teaspoons raspberry jam
250 g (8 oz/1½ cups) raspberries, thawed if frozen
315 ml (10 fl oz/1¼ cups) double (thick) cream
16 ratafias and angelica leaves, to decorate

Preheat oven to 150C (300F/Gas 2). Place milk and cream in a saucepan and bring almost to boiling point. Beat eggs and yolks together in a bowl, then pour milk mixture onto eggs, stirring well. Add sugar and rose water and stir until well blended. Divide mixture between 8 individual soufflé dishes. Stand dishes in a roasting tin half-filled with cold water. Cook in the oven for about 1 hour until custard has set. Remove dishes from water and leave until cold.

In a bowl, whisk egg, egg yolks and sugar until well blended. Bring milk and vanilla essence to the boil in a saucepan; pour onto eggs in bowl, stirring thoroughly. Rinse out saucepan and strain custard back into saucepan. Stirring continuously, cook over a gentle heat until thick, but do not boil. Leave until cold. Dip one sponge finger at a time into Madeira and brandy mixed together, spread with some jam and sandwich together with another dipped sponge finger. Place in a glass dish.

To make marinated fruit, mix together rose water, wine, icing sugar and rose petals in a bowl. Add the fruit and stir until well mixed. Cover with plastic wrap and chill until ready to serve. Turn custards out onto individual plates and spoon marinated fruit around base of each one.

Serves 8.

Repeat with remaining sponge fingers, Madeira, brandy and jam to cover base of dish. Pour remaining Madeira and brandy over top; cover with ⅔ raspberries. In a bowl, whip cream until softly peaking and fold ⅔ into cold custard. Pour over sponges and raspberries in bowl. Place remaining cream in a piping bag fitted with a star nozzle. Decorate trifle with piped cream, ratafias, angelica leaves and remaining raspberries. Chill.

Serves 8.

STRAWBERRY MILK JELLY

MAPLE BAVARIAN CREAM

500 ml (16 fl oz/2 cups) strawberry-flavoured drinking yogurt
3 teaspoons powdered gelatine
250 g (8 oz) strawberries

Pour yogurt into a bowl and chill.

1½ teaspoons powdered gelatine
3 tablespoons lemon juice and water, mixed
315 ml (10 fl oz/1¼ cups) double (thick) cream
5 tablespoons maple syrup
90 g (3 oz) crème fraîche
extra maple syrup for serving
langues de chat biscuits, to serve

Sprinkle gelatine over lemon juice and water in a small bowl and leave to soften for 2-3 minutes. In a bowl, whip cream lightly, adding half the maple syrup.

Sprinkle gelatine over 3 tablespoons water in a small bowl and leave to soften for 2-3 minutes. Stand the bowl in a saucepan of hot water and stir until the gelatine has dissolved. Whisk into chilled yogurt, then pour into a dampened 625 ml (20 fl oz/2½ cup) mould. Leave to set.

Stand gelatine bowl in a saucepan of hot water and stir until the gelatine has dissolved. Stir in remaining maple syrup, then pour into the cream, and whisk again until cream stands in soft peaks.

When ready to serve, slice strawberries. Turn out mould onto a serving plate and surround with strawberries.

Serves 4.

Note: For a softer texture jelly, increase quantity of yogurt to 625 ml (20 fl oz/2½ cups), but set in a bowl rather than a mould.

Variation: The jelly can be made in individual moulds, if preferred.

Fold crème fraîche into maple cream mixture. Spoon into individual glasses and chill until set. Top with extra maple syrup and serve with langues de chat biscuits.

Serves 4.

Note: Real maple syrup, as opposed to maple-flavoured syrup, is very expensive and not always easy to obtain. It is worth seeking out for this pudding, as it greatly improves the flavour of the cream.

COEURS À LA CRÈME

250 g (8 oz) ricotta or cottage cheese
30 g (1 oz/5 teaspoons) caster sugar
1 teaspoon lemon juice
315 ml (10 fl oz/1¼ cups) double (thick) cream
2 egg whites

TO SERVE: **fresh fruit or Raspberry Sauce (see page 91)
double (thick) cream**

Line 8 heart-shaped moulds with muslin.
Press cheese through a sieve into a bowl. Stir
in sugar and lemon juice.

In a separate bowl, whip cream until stiff. Stir
into cheese mixture. Whisk egg whites until
stiff, then fold into the cheese mixture.

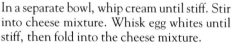

Spoon into moulds, place on 2 plates and
leave to drain overnight in the refrigerator.
To serve, unmould onto individual plates and
gently remove the muslin. Serve the hearts
with fresh fruit with cream handed separately,
or with whipped cream and Raspberry Sauce.

Serves 8.

Note: To add extra colour, decorate with
sprigs of redcurrants and blackcurrants.

ORANGE CARAMEL CREAM

125 g (4 oz/½ cup) granulated sugar
3 eggs
8 teaspoons caster sugar
315 ml (10 fl oz/1¼ cups) milk
3 teaspoons sweet orange oil
1 orange
fresh herbs, to decorate

Preheat oven to 180C (350F/Gas 4). Warm 4
china ramekin dishes or 4 dariole moulds. Put
granulated sugar and 3 tablespoons water into
a small saucepan and place over a low heat to
dissolve sugar. Increase heat and boil steadily,
without stirring, to a rich brown caramel.

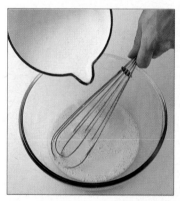

Divide between the dishes or moulds, tipping
them to cover bottom and sides with caramel.
Set aside. In a bowl, beat eggs and caster sugar
together. Heat milk until almost boiling,
then pour over egg mixture, beating all the
time. Stir in orange oil.

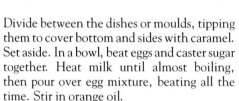

Strain mixture into dishes or moulds. Grate
orange peel finely, divide between dishes and
stir in. Place dishes in a roasting tin, pour in
boiling water to come halfway up the sides,
then bake in the oven for about 20 minutes,
until set. Cool in the dishes, then chill until
required. Turn out onto serving plates, and
decorate with segments cut from the grated
orange and herb leaves.

Serves 4.

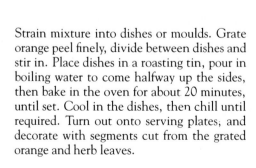

CARAMEL RICE

QUEEN OF PUDDINGS

75 g (2½ oz/⅓ cup) pudding rice, washed and drained
625 ml (20 fl oz/2½ cups) milk
1 vanilla pod
125 ml (4 fl oz/½ cup) single (light) cream
juice of 1 orange
caster sugar
orange peel strips, to decorate

Put rice, milk and vanilla pod into a saucepan and simmer on a very low heat for 45-60 minutes, until rice is soft and creamy.

500 ml (16 fl oz/2 cups) milk
155 ml (5 fl oz/⅔ cup) single cream
grated peel of 1 small lemon
90 g (3 oz/1½ cups) fresh white breadcrumbs
45 g (1½ oz/9 teaspoons) butter
250 g (8 oz/1¼ cups) caster sugar
3 small eggs, separated
3 tablespoons raspberry jam

Preheat oven to 180C (350F/Gas 4). Butter a 1.25 litre (40 fl oz/5 cup) pie dish. Put milk, cream and lemon peel in a saucepan.

Remove vanilla pod from mixture and stir in cream and orange juice. Spoon into an ovenproof gratin or soufflé dish. Leave to go cold, then refrigerate until ready to serve.

Heat milk mixture gently for 5 minutes, then remove from heat and leave to infuse for 5 minutes. Put breadcrumbs, butter and one-quarter of the sugar into a bowl and pour the warm milk on top. Stir until butter and sugar have dissolved. In a small bowl, beat egg yolks, then stir them into breadcrumb mixture. Turn into prepared pie dish and bake for 45-50 minutes, until set. Remove from oven and cool slightly. Warm raspberry jam in a pan and spread over pudding.

Cover top of pudding thickly and evenly with caster sugar. Place under a very hot grill until sugar topping has caramellized. Serve at once, decorated with orange peel.

Serves 4.

Note: Chill the pudding again before serving, if preferred, but serve within 2 hours.

Lower oven temperature to 160C (325F/Gas 3). In a large bowl, whisk egg whites until stiff, then fold in remaining sugar. Pile this meringue mixture onto pudding and return to oven for about 20 minutes, until meringue is crisp and golden. Serve warm or cold.

Serves 4.

Note: Sieve the warmed raspberry jam to remove pips, if desired.

BREAD & BUTTER PUDDING

125 g (4 oz/¾ cup) sultanas and currants, mixed
8 slices thin white bread, buttered
30 g (1 oz/2 tablespoons) candied fruit, chopped
caster sugar for sprinkling

CUSTARD: 1 egg yolk
315 ml (10 fl oz/1¼ cups) milk
155 ml (5 fl oz/⅔ cup) single (light) cream
1 vanilla pod
1 teaspoon caster sugar

Put sultanas and currants into a bowl and cover with water. Leave to swell. Preheat oven to 180C (350F/Gas 4). Grease a 1 litre (32 fl oz/4 cup) pie dish.

Cut crusts from bread and sandwich 4 slices together. Cut into 6 pieces and place in prepared pie dish. Drain fruit and scatter over bread with chopped candied fruit. Top with remaining bread, butter side up.

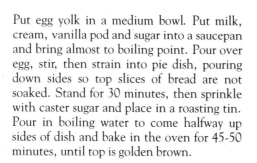

Put egg yolk in a medium bowl. Put milk, cream, vanilla pod and sugar into a saucepan and bring almost to boiling point. Pour over egg, stir, then strain into pie dish, pouring down sides so top slices of bread are not soaked. Stand for 30 minutes, then sprinkle with caster sugar and place in a roasting tin. Pour in boiling water to come halfway up sides of dish and bake in the oven for 45-50 minutes, until top is golden brown.

Serves 4.

CHARLOTTE RUSSE

16 sponge fingers
3 teaspoons powdered gelatine
4 egg yolks
90 g (3 oz/⅓ cup) caster sugar
625 ml (20 fl oz/2½ cups) whipping cream
1 vanilla pod, split open
315 ml (10 fl oz/1¼ cups) thick sour cream
185 g (6 oz) fresh raspberries
whipped cream, to decorate

Line the base of 1.1 litre (35 fl oz/4¼ cup) charlotte mould with greaseproof paper. Stand sponge fingers, pressing against each other, round sides of mould and trim to fit.

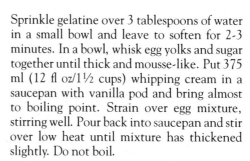

Sprinkle gelatine over 3 tablespoons of water in a small bowl and leave to soften for 2-3 minutes. In a bowl, whisk egg yolks and sugar together until thick and mousse-like. Put 375 ml (12 fl oz/1½ cups) whipping cream in a saucepan with vanilla pod and bring almost to boiling point. Strain over egg mixture, stirring well. Pour back into saucepan and stir over low heat until mixture has thickened slightly. Do not boil.

Strain into clean bowl and add soaked gelatine. Stir until dissolved. Cool, then stand bowl in larger bowl of iced water and stir until mixture thickens. Whip remaining cream with sour cream and fold into mixture. Pour into prepared mould, cover with plastic wrap and refrigerate overnight. When ready to serve, turn out onto serving plate, remove greaseproof paper and decorate with the raspberries and whipped cream. Tie a ribbon round pudding.

Serves 6-8.

ATHOLL BROSE

45 g (1½ oz/3 tablespoons) medium oatmeal
60 g (2 oz/⅓ cup) whole blanched almonds
315 ml (10 fl oz/1¼ cups) double (thick) cream
60 ml (2 fl oz/¼ cup) whisky
90 g (3 oz/¼ cup) orange flower honey
1 tablespoon lemon juice

Toast oatmeal under a medium-hot grill until evenly browned. Toast the almonds in the same way, then chop them finely.

In a large bowl, whip cream to soft peaks, then gradually whisk in whisky, honey and lemon juice.

Fold oatmeal and half the chopped almonds into creamy mixture and spoon into 4 glasses. Chill in the refrigerator. When ready to serve, sprinkle remaining almonds on top of each pudding.

Serves 4.

Note: This traditional Scottish dessert is very rich and is perfect for a dinner party.

YOGURT FUDGE CREAM

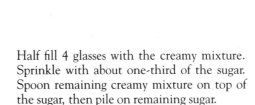

315 ml (10 fl oz/1¼ cups) whipping cream
250 g (8 oz/1 cup) natural yogurt
250 g (8 oz/1½ cups) brown sugar
fresh strawberries or raspberries, to serve, if desired

In a large bowl, whip cream to stiff peaks. Fold in the yogurt.

Half fill 4 glasses with the creamy mixture. Sprinkle with about one-third of the sugar. Spoon remaining creamy mixture on top of the sugar, then pile on remaining sugar.

Chill in the refrigerator overnight. Serve puddings on their own, or with fresh strawberries or raspberries, if desired.

Serves 4.

Note: The brown sugar dissolves and forms a fudgy layer in these puddings. They must be prepared a day in advance to allow for this.

RICE & FRUIT MOULD

AMARETTI CHEESE WHIP

100 g (3½ oz/½ cup plus 1 tablespoon) pudding rice
940 ml (30 fl oz/3¾ cups) milk
caster sugar, to taste
grated peel and juice of 1 orange
3 teaspoons powdered gelatine
250 g (8 oz) mixed fresh fruit, such as grapes, bananas
  and strawberries
2 tablespoons whipping cream
2 egg whites
Raspberry Sauce (see page 91), to serve

Wash rice, put in saucepan with milk and simmer for 40-60 minutes, until creamy. Sweeten rice with caster sugar and stir in grated orange peel.

Sprinkle gelatine over orange juice in a small bowl and leave to soften for 2-3 minutes. Stand bowl in saucepan of hot water and stir until gelatine has dissolved. Stir into rice. Leave to cool. To prepare fruit, halve and seed grapes, finely slice bananas and cut strawberries into quarters. Reserve a few pieces for decoration and fold remainder into rice. In a bowl, whip cream lightly.

In a separate bowl, whisk egg whites stiffly. Fold cream, then egg whites into rice mixture. Turn into a glass serving bowl or a lightly oiled ring mould and chill until set. Turn out of mould, if using, decorate with reserved fruit and serve with the sauce.

Serves 4-6.

Note: Turn moulded puddings out onto a wet serving plate. The pudding will then slide easily over the plate, so it can be centred.

60 g (2 oz/¼ cup) caster sugar
2 eggs, separated
315 g (10 oz/1¼ cups) mascarpone cream cheese
finely grated peel of 1 tangerine
125 g (4 oz) mixed glacé fruit, chopped
30 g (1 oz) Amaretti biscuits
4 teaspoons Amaretti liqueur
155 ml (5 fl oz/⅔ cup) double (thick) cream
chopped glacé fruit and Amaretti biscuits, to decorate

Place sugar and egg yolks in a bowl over a saucepan of simmering water and whisk until mixture leaves a trail when whisk is lifted.

Stir in mascarpone cheese, tangerine peel and glacé fruit. Break Amaretti biscuits into pieces and add to mixture; stir in liqueur. Whisk egg whites in a bowl until stiff. Place cream in another bowl and whip until thick. Add egg whites and cream to cream cheese mixture and fold in carefully until mixture is evenly blended. Cover with plastic wrap and chill until required.

Just before serving, divide mixture between 6-8 small glasses and decorate with chopped glacé fruit and Amaretti biscuits.

Serves 6-8.

FESTIVE CHEESECAKE

BASE: 60 g (2 oz/¼ cup) butter
3 teaspoons golden syrup
220 g (7 oz/2 cups) plain biscuit crumbs

FILLING AND TOPPING: 375 g (12 oz/1½ cups) cream
   cheese
155 ml (5 fl oz/⅔ cup) fromage frais
2 eggs, separated
4 teaspoons grenadine syrup
90 ml (3 fl oz/⅓ cup) Marsala
5 teaspoons powdered gelatine
1 star fruit, sliced
2 figs, sliced
10 kumquats, sliced
12 melon balls
10 green and black grapes, halved and seeded

Gently heat butter and syrup in a saucepan
until melted. Stir in biscuit crumbs and press
onto base of a 22.5 cm (9 in) spring-form tin.
In a bowl, beat cream cheese, fromage frais,
egg yolks, 3 teaspoons grenadine syrup and 6
teaspoons Marsala until smooth. Sprinkle
gelatine over 9 teaspoons water in a small
bowl; leave to soften. Stand bowl in saucepan
of hot water and stir until dissolved and quite
hot. Stir into cheese mixture and leave until
thickened. Stiffly whisk egg whites; fold into
mixture.

Pour into tin, shake to level; chill until set. In
a bowl, place prepared fruit. Heat remaining
grenadine and Marsala in a saucepan until
hot, but not boiling. Pour over fruits and
leave until cold. Drain liquor into a saucepan
and arrange fruit over top of cheesecake. Boil
liquid until syrupy and brush over fruit to
glaze. Serve cut into slices.

Serves 8.

AUSTRIAN CURD CHEESECAKE

60 g (2 oz/¼ cup) butter, softened
140 g (4½ oz/⅔ cup) caster sugar
280 g (9 oz) curd cheese, sieved
2 eggs, separated
60 g (2 oz/½ cup) ground almonds
60 g (2 oz/⅓ cup) fine semolina
juice and grated peel of 1 small lemon
icing sugar
Raspberry Sauce (see page 91) or Hot Lemon Sauce
   (see page 93), to serve

Preheat oven to 190C (375F/Gas 5). Butter a
20 cm (8 in) cake tin and dust out with flour.
In a large bowl, cream butter, sugar and
cheese until soft and fluffy.

Beat egg yolks into mixture, then fold in
almonds, semolina and lemon juice and peel.
In a separate bowl, whisk egg whites stiffly
and carefully fold into the cheese mixture.

Turn mixture into prepared tin and bake in
the oven for about 50 minutes, until golden
brown and springy to touch. Cool for 20
minutes in tin, then turn out and dust with
icing sugar. Serve warm or cold, with
Raspberry or Hot Lemon Sauce.

Serves 6.

Note: For a pretty pattern, place a doily on
the cake, then dust with icing sugar. Remove
doily and serve.

OEUFS À LA NEIGE

GRAPEFRUIT CHEESECAKE

4 eggs, separated
scant ½ teaspoon cornflour
90 g (3 oz/⅓ cup) caster sugar
125 ml (4 fl oz/½ cup) milk
315 ml (10 fl oz/1¼ cups) single (light) cream
1 vanilla pod
1 tablespoon orange flower water
1 tablespoon toasted, flaked almonds
orange peel strips, to decorate

In a bowl, cream egg yolks with cornflour and one-third of the caster sugar. Place milk, cream and vanilla pod in a saucepan and scald (bring to near boiling point).

Pour the hot milk over the egg yolks, whisking all the time. Place bowl over a saucepan of simmering water and cook gently, stirring, until it is the consistency of double cream. Cool, remove vanilla pod and stir in orange flower water. In a large bowl, whisk egg whites until stiff, add remaining sugar and whisk again.

Fill a large saucepan with water and bring to simmering point. Put spoonfuls of meringue mixture, a few at a time, into water and poach for 5 minutes, turning carefully once. (There should be enough meringue for 4 spoonfuls per portion.) Drain on absorbent kitchen paper and cool. Pour most of the custard into a glass serving bowl and arrange meringue puffs on top. Drizzle the remaining custard over meringues, then sprinkle with flaked almonds. Decorate with orange peel.

Serves 4.

250 g (8 oz) semi-sweet wheatmeal biscuits
125 g (4 oz/½ cup) butter, melted
2 pink grapefruit
3 teaspoons powdered gelatine
250 g (8 oz) cream cheese
155 ml (5 fl oz/⅔ cup) single (light) cream
2 tablespoons caster sugar
juice and grated peel of 1 lemon
4 egg whites

Crush biscuits to crumbs and mix with the melted butter.

Press two-thirds of the crumb mixture over base of a 22.5 cm (9 in) loose-bottomed or springform tin and chill. Cut off peel and pith from grapefruit, holding over a bowl to catch juice. Cut out segments from between membranes and set aside. Squeeze membranes into bowl to extract juice. Sprinkle gelatine over grapefruit juice and leave for 2-3 minutes to soften. Stand in a saucepan of hot water and stir until gelatine has dissolved. In a bowl, beat cream cheese, cream and sugar. Stir in gelatine, lemon juice and peel.

Whisk egg whites in a large bowl until stiff. Fold into creamy mixture. Pour over crumb mixture and return tin to refrigerator to set. To serve, remove cheesecake from tin and decorate with grapefruit segments. Press remaining crumbs evenly into sides of cake.

Serves 6-8.

Note: If liked, salt can be sprinkled onto the grapefruit to act as an alkali, making the grapefruit less acidic, so less sugar is needed to sweeten the fruit.

SOUFFLÉS, OMELETTES, MOUSSES & MERINGUES

HOT CHOCOLATE SOUFFLÉ

RED BERRY SOUFFLÉ

2 tablespoons caster sugar
125 g (4 oz) plain (dark) chocolate
2 tablespoons brandy or coffee
4 eggs, separated, plus 2 extra whites
icing sugar, to serve

Preheat oven to 200C (400F/Gas 6). Butter a 1 litre (32 fl oz/4 cup) soufflé dish and dust out with 1 tablespoon caster sugar. Break chocolate into pieces and put into a double boiler or a bowl set over a saucepan of simmering water with the brandy or coffee.

Set over medium heat and stir until smooth. Take care not to overheat the chocolate or it will lose its gloss and become very thick and difficult to combine with other ingredients. Remove from heat and beat in egg yolks with remaining caster sugar. In a bowl, whisk egg whites until stiff but not dry. Fold 1 tablespoon into chocolate mixture, then scrape into egg whites and quickly fold together using a metal spoon.

Pour into prepared soufflé dish, place on a baking sheet and bake in the oven for 15-18 minutes, until risen and just set. Serve immediately, dusted with icing sugar.

Serves 4.

Note: You could serve Dark Chocolate sauce (see page 92) or Bitter Mocha Sauce (see page 93) with the soufflé.

30 g (1 oz/6 teaspoons) butter
125 g (4 oz/½ cup) caster sugar, plus 1 extra tablespoon
250 g (8 oz) mixed soft red fruits, fresh or frozen,
   thawed if frozen
1 tablespoon Fraise liqueur or crème de cassis
5 egg whites
icing sugar, to serve

Preheat oven to 180C (350F/Gas 4). Use the butter to grease a 1 litre (32 fl oz/4 cup) soufflé dish or 6 individual dishes, then dust out with 1 tablespoon caster sugar.

Purée fruit, liqueur and remaining caster sugar together in a blender or food processor. Turn into a bowl. In a separate bowl, whisk egg whites until stiff, but not dry. Fold 1 tablespoon into fruit purée, then tip purée onto whites and fold together carefully, using a metal spoon.

Spoon mixture into prepared soufflé dish, place on a baking sheet and bake in the oven for 25-30 minutes for the large soufflé; 15-20 minutes for the individual soufflés, until risen and just set. Dust with a little icing sugar and serve immediately.

Serves 6.

COFFEE CHIFFON DESSERTS

60 g (2 oz/¼ cup) butter
9 teaspoons golden syrup
220 g (7 oz/2 cups) crunchy oat biscuit crumbs

FILLING: 30 g (1 oz/9 teaspoons) cornflour
60 g (2 oz/¼ cup) caster sugar
3 teaspoons instant coffee
315 ml (10 fl oz/1¼ cups) milk
2 eggs, separated
5 teaspoons powdered gelatine
315 ml (10 fl oz/1¼ cups) whipping cream
155 ml (5 fl oz/⅔ cup) double (thick) cream, whipped
  and liqueur chocolate coffee beans, to decorate

Melt butter and syrup in a saucepan; mix in biscuit crumbs. Divide between 8 tiny moulds, lined with plastic wrap; press evenly over bases and sides. Chill. Blend cornflour with sugar, coffee and milk in a saucepan. Bring to boil, stirring; cook for 2 minutes. Remove from heat; beat in egg yolks. Sprinkle gelatine over 9 teaspoons hot water in a small bowl; leave to soften. Stand bowl in a pan of hot water; stir until dissolved. Stir into coffee mixture; leave until thick but not set.

Stiffly whisk egg whites; whip cream until thick. Fold cream and egg whites evenly into coffee mixture. Divide mixture between the moulds, filling each to the top. Cover and chill until set. To serve, invert moulds onto serving plates and remove plastic wrap. Place remaining cream in a piping bag fitted with a star nozzle and pipe around top and base of moulds. Decorate with coffee beans.

Makes 8.

SOUFFLÉ LIME & CHOC LAYER

4 eggs, separated
90 g (3 oz/⅓ cup) caster sugar
3 teaspoons powdered gelatine
finely grated peel and juice of 1 lime
60 g (2 oz) plain (dark) chocolate, melted
315 ml (10 fl oz/1¼ cups) whipping cream
chocolate curls and lime peel, to decorate

Place egg yolks and sugar in a bowl over a saucepan of simmering water. Whisk until pale and thick. Remove bowl from saucepan, continue to whisk until mixture leaves a trail when whisk is lifted.

Sprinkle gelatine over 9 teaspoons water in a small bowl and leave to soften for 2-3 minutes. Stand bowl in a saucepan of hot water and stir until dissolved and quite hot. Stir gelatine into mixture until well blended. Pour ½ quantity of mixture into another bowl. Stir lime peel and juice into one mixture and chocolate into remaining mixture. Stir each until well blended. Whisk egg whites in a bowl until stiff. Whip cream until thick.

Add ½ quantity egg whites and cream to each mixture and fold in carefully until evenly blended. Spoon alternate spoonfuls of each mixture into 8 small glasses. Leave until set, then decorate with chocolate curls and lime peel.

Serves 8.

— DIJON SURPRISE OMELETTE —

| 6 eggs |
| 6 teaspoons caster sugar |
| 2 almond macaroon biscuits, crushed |
| 6 teaspoons single (light) cream |
| 30 g (1 oz/6 teaspoons) butter |
| 5 tablespoons blackcurrant jam |
| 30 g (1 oz/¼ cup) finely chopped walnuts |
| TOPPING: |
| 2 egg whites |
| 125 g (4 oz/½ cup) caster sugar |
| 6 teaspoons icing sugar, sifted |

Preheat oven to 220C (425F/Gas 7). In a bowl, beat eggs, sugar, crushed biscuits and cream until thick and creamy. Melt half the butter in a 17.5 cm (7 in) omelette pan, pour in half egg mixture and cook over low heat until just set. Lift on to a warm ovenproof plate, then repeat with remaining egg mixture.

Warm jam in a small saucepan and stir in walnuts. Spread mixture on first omelette and top with other omelette. In a bowl, whisk egg whites to stiff peaks, then fold in caster sugar. Carefully pipe or spread over omelettes, making sure they are completely covered. Sprinkle with icing sugar and bake in the oven for 3 minutes, until meringue is lightly coloured. Serve at once.

Serves 4.

— BAKED ALASKA OMELETTE —

| 625 ml (20 fl oz) block vanilla ice cream |
| 250 g (8 oz) raspberries or strawberries |
| 6 teaspoons kirsch |
| 6 teaspoons caster sugar |
| 3 eggs, separated |
| one 17.5 cm (7 in) oblong sponge cake |
| caster sugar for sprinkling. |
| strawberry halves, to decorate |

Make sure ice cream is very hard before preparing recipe. Preheat oven to 220C (425F/Gas 7).

Leave raspberries whole, or slice strawberries, if using. Put into a bowl with kirsch and half sugar and leave to stand while preparing recipe.

Beat egg yolks with remaining sugar until thick and creamy. Whisk whites to stiff peaks and fold into yolks.

Place sponge cake on a large ovenproof serving plate. Spoon over fruit and soaking liquid and top with block of ice cream, cutting the ice cream to fit, if necessary.

Quickly cover ice cream and sponge cake with egg mixture, making sure the top and sides are completely covered. Sprinkle with caster sugar and bake for 3 minutes, until light golden. Decorate with strawberry halves, then serve at once, cut into wedges.

Serves 6.

SOUFFLÉ OMELETTE

3 eggs, separated
1 tablespoon single (light) cream
2 teaspoons caster sugar
15 g (½ oz/3 teaspoons) butter
6 teaspoons raspberry jam
icing sugar

Preheat oven to 200C (400F/Gas 6). In a bowl, beat egg yolks, cream and sugar lightly. In a separate larger bowl, whisk egg whites until stiff. Add yolk mixture to whisked whites and carefully fold together.

– SUMMER SOUFFLÉ OMELETTE –

185 g (6 oz) prepared soft fruits, such as blackcurrants, redcurrants, raspberries, strawberries

3 tablespoons crème de cassis or water

3 teaspoons caster sugar

3 teaspoons arrowroot

one 3-egg Basic Soufflé Omelette, see right

1 tablespoon icing sugar, sifted

soft fruit and leaves, to decorate

Prepare filling before making omelette. Put fruit in a saucepan with crème de cassis or water and sugar.

Heat gently until juices run. Remove from heat. Mix arrowroot with a little water and stir in. Return to heat and cook, stirring, until thick. Leave filling to cool.

Make omelette and place on a warm serving plate. Spoon fruit mixture over half omelette and fold over, then sprinkle with icing sugar. Decorate with soft fruit and leaves, if desired, and serve at once.

Serves 2.

Melt butter in an omelette pan over medium heat and pour soufflé mixture into pan. Spread it evenly and cook for about 1 minute, until brown underneath. Put pan in oven for 5 minutes, until top is set. Meanwhile, heat 2 skewers either in a gas flame or under a very hot grill until they are red hot and glowing.

In a small saucepan, warm jam slightly. Remove omelette from oven and quickly spread with jam. Fold over and transfer to a serving plate. Sift icing sugar thickly over omelette, then holding the skewers with thick oven gloves, mark a criss-cross pattern in the icing sugar by pressing the skewers into it. Cut omelette in half and serve.

Serves 2.

AMARETTI MOUSSE

MANGO MOUSSE

100 g (3½ oz/½ cup) whole blanched almonds
60 g (2 oz) Amaretti biscuits
3 eggs, plus 2 extra yolks
90 g (3 oz/⅓ cup) caster sugar
3 teaspoons powdered gelatine
2 tablespoons lemon juice
1-2 tablespoons Amaretto or Kirsch
315 ml (10fl oz/1¼ cups) whipping cream

Toast nuts under a medium grill to brown. Put with biscuits in food processor fitted with metal blade and process to crumbs.

440 g (14 oz) can mangoes
juice of ½ lemon
1-2 tablespoons caster sugar
3 teaspoons powdered gelatine
315 ml (10 fl oz/1¼ cups) whipping cream
fresh mango slices and lemon peel strips, to decorate

Drain mangoes well and purée flesh with lemon juice in a blender or food processor. Pour into a bowl and sweeten to taste with caster sugar.

In a bowl, whisk eggs, extra yolks and sugar together until thick and mousse-like. Sprinkle gelatine over lemon juice in a small bowl and leave to soften for 2-3 minutes. Stand bowl in saucepan of hot water and stir until gelatine has dissolved. Add to egg mixture with liqueur and three-quarters of nut and biscuit mixture. Whip cream stiffly and fold two-thirds into mixture.

Sprinkle gelatine over 5 tablespoons water in a small bowl and leave to soften for 2-3 minutes. Stand bowl in a saucepan of hot water and stir until gelatine has dissolved. Stir into purée, then put in a cool place until on point of setting. In a bowl, whip cream lightly and fold into mango mixture.

Pour mixture into a 1 litre (32 fl oz/ 4 cup) soufflé dish and put in refrigerator to set. Just before serving, decorate with piped rosettes of reserved whipping cream and sprinkle remaining nuts and biscuits on top.

Serves 6-8.

Note: Amaretto is a very sweet liqueur made from almonds. Kirsch gives a more subtle flavour and makes the dessert less sweet.

Pour mixture into a glass serving bowl or individual glasses and chill until set. Decorate with fresh mango slices and lemon peel just before serving.

Serves 4.

Note: When folding whipped cream and/or egg whites into gelatine mixtures, it is essential that the base mixture is on the point of setting. If folded in too soon, the mixture will separate out to jelly on the bottom and froth on top.

PASSION FRUIT MOUSSE

12 passion fruit
juice and grated peel of 1 large orange
5 eggs
125 g (4 oz/½ cup) caster sugar
3 teaspoons powdered gelatine
315 ml (10 fl oz/1¼ cups) whipping cream

Cut passion fruit in half, scoop out flesh and place in a saucepan with orange juice. Heat gently for 2-3 minutes, cool and then chill in the refrigerator.

In a large bowl, whisk orange peel, eggs and sugar until thick and mousse-like. Sprinkle gelatine over 3 tablespoons water in a small bowl and leave to soften for 2-3 minutes. Stand bowl in a saucepan of hot water and stir until gelatine has dissolved. Add to egg mixture. Sieve chilled passion fruit mixture and stir half into mousse. Return remainder to refrigerator.

In a bowl, whip cream lightly and fold into mousse mixture. Turn into a soufflé dish or glass serving bowl and chill until required. Serve reserved passion fruit mixture separately as a sauce.

Serves 6.

Note: Put passion fruit into a bowl with unripe fruits, and the unripe fruits will ripen more speedily.

MINTY CHOCOLATE MOUSSE

185 g (6 oz) plain (dark) chocolate
315 ml (10 fl oz/1¼ cups) double (thick) cream
1 egg
pinch of salt
few drops peppermint essence

TO DECORATE: mint leaves
1 small egg white
caster sugar
grated chocolate

Break chocolate into small pieces and put into a blender or food processor fitted with a metal blade.

Heat cream in a small saucepan until almost boiling. Pour over chocolate and blend for 1 minute. Add egg, salt and peppermint essence and blend for 1 minute more. Pour into individual ramekin dishes or chocolate cups and refrigerate overnight.

To make the decoration, wash and dry mint leaves. Lightly whisk egg white in a shallow bowl and dip in mint leaves to cover. Dip them into caster sugar, shake off any excess and leave to harden on greaseproof paper. Place on each mousse just before serving and sprinkle with grated chocolate.

Serves 4-6.

Note: Peppermint essence has a very strong flavour; use it sparingly.

MERINGUES WITH HONEY

CHOCOLATE MERINGUES

2 egg whites
125 g (4 oz/½ cup) caster sugar

TO SERVE: **2 tablespoons clear honey**
2 tablespoons toasted flaked almonds
315 ml (10 fl oz/1¼ cups) whipping cream

Preheat oven to 150C (300F/Gas 2). Line baking sheets with silicone paper. Put egg whites into a large bowl and whisk until stiff, but not dry.

1 quantity of Meringue mixture (see left)
125 g (4 oz) plain (dark) chocolate
315 ml (10 fl oz/1¼ cups) whipping cream
fresh strawberries, hulled, to decorate

Preheat oven to 150C (300F/Gas 2). Line 2 baking sheets with silicone paper. Use meringue mixture to pipe 12 shells onto prepared baking sheets. Cook and cool as described (see left).

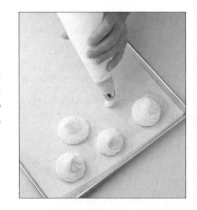

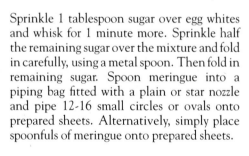

Sprinkle 1 tablespoon sugar over egg whites and whisk for 1 minute more. Sprinkle half the remaining sugar over the mixture and fold in carefully, using a metal spoon. Then fold in remaining sugar. Spoon meringue into a piping bag fitted with a plain or star nozzle and pipe 12-16 small circles or ovals onto prepared sheets. Alternatively, simply place spoonfuls of meringue onto prepared sheets.

Break chocolate into squares and melt with 2 tablespoons water in the top of a double boiler or a bowl set over a saucepan of simmering water. Stir occasionally, until melted and smooth. Dip the flat underside of meringues into melted chocolate to cover. Set on their sides for the chocolate to harden.

Bake meringues in the oven for 1-1½ hours, until crisp on the outside. Cool on a wire rack. When cold, pile onto a serving plate, dribble honey over the top and sprinkle with toasted flaked almonds. Whip cream until stiff and serve separately.

Makes 12-16 shells.

Note: An electric or hand whisk can be used to make meringues. Separate eggs carefully so there is no yolk with the white.

Whip cream, place in piping bag fitted with a star nozzle and pipe onto 6 shells. Sandwich in pairs with remaining 6 shells. Place meringues in paper serving cases, or on individual plates, and decorate with slices of strawberries.

Serves 6.

Note: A few drops of red food colouring can be added to basic meringue mixture to colour it pink, if desired.

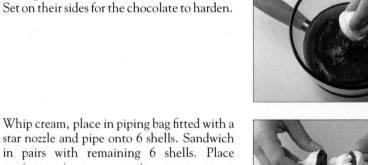

GINGER MARRONS GLACÉS

FESTIVE MERINGUES

PAVLOVA: 3 egg whites
220 g (7 oz/1 cup) caster sugar
1 teaspoon white wine vinegar
1 teaspoon orange flower water
1 teaspoon cornflour

FILLING: 315 ml (10 fl oz/1¼ cups) whipping cream
3 pieces preserved stem ginger in syrup
vanilla ice cream
10 whole marrons glacés, each cut into 8 pieces

Preheat oven to 140C (275F/Gas 1). Line 3 baking sheets with non-stick baking paper, mark ten 8 cm (3 in) circles and invert paper.

Whisk egg whites in a bowl until stiff. Gradually add sugar, whisking well after each addition until thick. In a bowl, blend together the vinegar, orange flower water and cornflour. Add to meringue and whisk until very thick and glossy. Place meringue in a large piping bag fitted with a small star nozzle. Pipe a shell edging around the marked lines on the paper, then fill in centres with a thin layer of meringue. Pipe a second shell edging on top of the first edge.

Bake in the oven for 45 minutes. Turn off oven and leave in oven to cool. Remove when cold; store in an airtight container until required. Whip cream in a bowl until thick, place ½ in a piping bag fitted with a nozzle. Chop the ginger and fold into remaining cream and spread over each pavlova. Just before serving, top each with scoops of ice cream, whipped cream and a marron glacé.

Serves 10.

MERINGUE: 2 egg whites
125 g (4 oz/½ cup) caster sugar

TOPPING: 250 g (8 oz) mixed glacé fruit, chopped
8 teaspoons Strega liqueur
250 ml (8 fl oz/1 cup) double (thick) cream
60 ml (2 fl oz/¼ cup) Greek yogurt
1 star fruit, thinly sliced, to decorate

Preheat oven to 110C (225F/Gas ¼). Line 2 baking sheets with non-stick paper. Draw 10 oval shapes on each, using a 6 cm (2½ in) oval cutter. Invert paper.

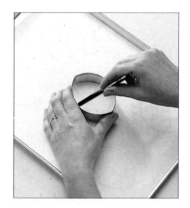

In a bowl, whisk egg whites until stiff. Whisk in sugar a little at a time, whisking thoroughly until thick. Place mixture in a large piping bag fitted with a medium star nozzle. Pipe shells of meringue around each oval shape, then fill in centres, making sure there are no gaps. Bake in the oven for 1½-2 hours until meringues are dry and crisp; lift off paper. Cool and store in an airtight tin until required.

In a bowl, mix fruit with Strega; cover and leave until required. Whip cream and yogurt together in a bowl until thick, add ⅔ of glacé fruit and all the liqueur and fold in until just mixed. Spoon mixture onto each meringue oval and decorate with slices of star fruit and remaining glacé fruit.

Makes 20.

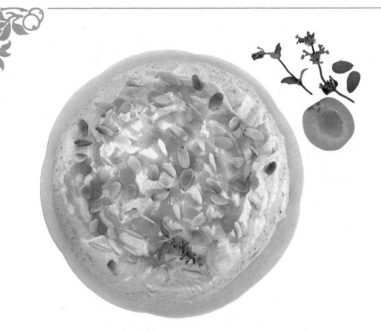

DACQUOISE

155 g (5 oz/1 cup) whole blanched almonds
5 egg whites
315 g (10 oz/1½ cups) caster sugar
185 g (6 oz/2¾ cups) dried apricots
juice of 1 lemon
375 ml (12 fl oz/1½ cups) whipping cream
toasted flaked almonds, to decorate

Preheat oven to 150C (300F/Gas 2). Line a baking sheet with silicone paper. Toast almonds under a medium grill to brown evenly. Cool, then grind finely in a coffee grinder or food processor. Set aside.

In a large bowl, whisk egg whites until stiff, but not dry. Sprinkle over 2 tablespoons of the caster sugar and whisk for a further 1 minute. Fold in remaining sugar with ground almonds, using a metal spoon. Spoon meringue onto lined baking sheet and spread evenly to a 25 cm (10 in) circle. Bake in the oven for 1½-2 hours, until dry and biscuit coloured. Peel off paper and cool meringue on a wire rack.

Put apricots and lemon juice into a saucepan, cover with water and simmer over medium heat for about 30 minutes, until tender. Cool, then purée apricots with a little cooking liquid in a blender or food processor to make a thick purée. Whip cream stiffly and fold half the purée into it. Pile onto meringue and dribble remaining purée, thinned with a little more cooking liquid, over top. Sprinkle with flaked almonds to decorate.

Serves 6-8.

MINI PAVLOVAS

2 egg whites
345 g (11 oz/1½ cups) caster sugar
½ teaspoon vinegar
½ teaspoon cornflour
4 tablespoons boiling water

TO SERVE: 1 quantity of Citrus Flummery (see page 9) or whipped cream and Blackcurrant Sauce (see page 90)
orange peel, if desired

Preheat oven to 120C (250F/Gas ½). Line 2 baking sheets with silicone paper. In a large bowl, stir together egg whites, sugar, vinegar and cornflour.

Add boiling water and whisk with an electric whisk until mixture is white and thick – this takes a good 10 minutes. Place 8 large spoonfuls on the prepared baking sheets and spread out to 10 cm (4 in) diameter circles. Make a slight depression in the centre of each, using the back of a spoon.

Bake pavlovas in the oven for about 30 minutes, until crisp on the outside – they are like marshmallow on the inside. Remove from baking sheets and cool on wire trays. For serving, fill the centres with Citrus Flummery, spooning or piping it into the pavlovas. Alternatively, fill with whipped cream with Blackcurrant Sauce poured over the top. Decorate with orange peel cut into shapes, if desired.

Serves 8.

PANCAKES & WAFFLES

BASIC CRÊPES

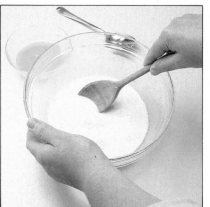

125 g (4 oz/1 cup) plain flour
pinch of salt
2 eggs
315 ml (10 fl oz/1¼ cups) milk
3 teaspoons butter, melted
vegetable oil or lard for cooking
lemon juice and sugar, or
warmed jam

Sift flour and salt into a bowl. Make a well in centre and add eggs and a little milk. Beat, working in all flour. Beat in remaining milk and butter.

Heat a little vegetable oil or lard in a 17.5 cm (7 in) crêpe pan, barely covering the base. Pour in 2–3 tablespoons batter, tilting the pan so the batter covers the base thinly and evenly. Cook over high heat for about 1 minute, until lightly browned underneath.

Turn crêpe with a palette knife and cook other side for about 30 seconds. Remove from pan and keep warm, then continue until all the batter is used. Serve with lemon juice and sugar or warmed jam.

Makes 8.

CRÊPE RIBBONS

1 quantity of Basic Crêpes (see left)
oil for deep frying

TO SERVE: **icing sugar**
Raspberry Sauce, Blackcurrant Sauce or Crème à la Vanille (see pages 90 and 91)

Leave the cooked pancakes to cool.

Cut cold pancakes into ribbons or strips. Heat a pan of oil for deep frying; test the temperature by dropping in a small piece of pancake. It should sizzle furiously. Fry the ribbons in batches, until crisp and golden. Remove with a slotted spoon and drain on crumpled absorbent kitchen paper. Keep warm while cooking the remainder.

Pile the warm crêpe ribbons onto a serving dish, dredge with icing sugar and serve immediately with chosen sauce.

Serves 4.

Note: Pancakes for this recipe can be made a day in advance and kept, wrapped in foil, in the refrigerator, or they may be frozen. Thaw the pancakes for 1-2 hours at room temperature before frying.

— HONEYED BANANA TOPPING —

3 bananas
2 teaspoons lemon juice
4 tablespoons clear honey
pinch of grated nutmeg

Peel the bananas and slice into strips. Put them into a bowl, add lemon juice and toss well so the slices are coated, to prevent browning.

Put honey into a small saucepan and warm over low heat. Add bananas and heat through until just warm, then season with nutmeg. Serve with any crêpes.

Serves 4.

RASPBERRY TOPPING —

375 g (12 oz) frozen raspberries, thawed
30 g (1 oz/6 teaspoons) sugar
3 teaspoons cornflour
raspberry leaves, to decorate, if desired

Drain raspberries and put juice into a small saucepan with 155 ml (5 fl oz/ ⅔ cup) water and sugar and bring to the boil. Mix cornflour with 6 teaspoons cold water in a bowl, then add the boiling liquid, stirring well. Return to pan and bring to the boil over low heat until mixture thickens, stirring constantly.

Remove from heat and stir in raspberries. Return to heat and heat gently without breaking up fruit. Serve with any crêpes, decorated with raspberry leaves, if desired.

Serves 4.

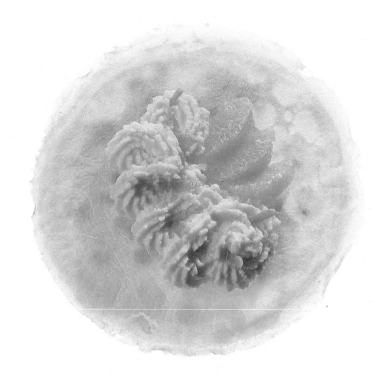

— BANANA CREAM TOPPING —

155 ml (5 fl oz/⅔ cup) whipping cream
2 large bananas
30 g (1 oz/2 tablespoons) icing sugar
2 teaspoons lemon juice
½ teaspoon grated nutmeg
pecan nuts and extra nutmeg, to decorate, if desired

In a bowl, whip the cream to soft peaks. Mash the bananas in a separate bowl with the sugar and lemon juice.

Fold the cream into the banana mixture and add the nutmeg. Put into a serving bowl. Cover and chill until ready to serve. If desired, serve decorated with pecan nuts and extra nutmeg.

Serves 4.

— ORANGE LIQUEUR TOPPING —

60 g (2 oz/¼ cup) butter, softened
125 g (4 oz/¾ cup) icing sugar
finely grated peel and juice of 1 orange
6 teaspoons orange-flavoured liqueur
orange segments and lemon peel strips, to decorate

Cream the butter and icing sugar in a bowl until light and fluffy.

Gradually beat orange peel and juice into the butter mixture, then gradually add the orange liqueur, beating until soft and creamy. Turn into a serving bowl and chill for at least 30 minutes before serving. To serve, pipe or spoon onto a flat crêpe. Decorate with orange segments and lemon peel strips.

Serves 4.

Note: For children, the orange-flavoured liqueur can be replaced with additional orange juice.

FRESH LEMON TOPPING

finely grated peel and juice of 2 lemons
60 g (2 oz/¼ cup) sugar
6 teaspoons cornflour
6 teaspoons lemon curd
lemon peel strips, to decorate

Put lemon peel and juice into a saucepan with 250 ml (8 fl oz/1 cup) water and the sugar. Heat gently until the sugar has dissolved.

Mix the cornflour with 60 ml (2 fl oz/¼ cup) water in a bowl. Add a little of the hot liquid and stir well, then return to the pan with the lemon curd. Stir over low heat until the sauce is thick and glossy. Turn into a warm serving bowl. To serve, decorate with lemon peel strips.

Serves 4.

JAMAICAN BANANA TOPPING

125 g (4 oz/½ cup) butter
125 g (4 oz/¾ cup) dark moist brown sugar
finely grated peel and juice of 1 lemon
3 medium bananas
6 teaspoons dark rum
lemon twists and lemon peel strips, to decorate

Put butter and sugar into a saucepan and stir over low heat until the butter has melted. Stir the lemon peel and juice into the butter and continue simmering for 1 minute.

Peel the bananas and slice thinly. Stir into the sugar mixture. Warm through for 2 minutes, then remove from heat and stir in rum. Turn into a warm serving bowl. To serve, decorate with lemon twists and lemon peel strips.

Serves 4.

APPLE PANCAKES

125 g (4 oz/1 cup) plain flour
pinch of salt
250 ml (8 fl oz/1 cup) milk and water, mixed
2 eggs
1 tablespoon oil or melted butter
3 well-flavoured eating apples
2 teaspoons lemon juice
1 tablespoon brandy
2 teaspoons caster sugar

Make pancake batter as described on page 34 and leave to stand for 30 minutes.

Peel and core apples and slice very finely onto a plate. Sprinkle with lemon juice and brandy. Heat a 15-17.5 cm (6-7 in) heavy-based frying pan and grease lightly. Pour in 1 tablespoon batter and roll pan to spread it evenly. Put a few apple slices over pancake, then spoon a little more batter over apple. Cook for 2-3 minutes, until batter is almost set. Hold pan under a hot grill to finish cooking batter.

Turn pancake out onto a plate and serve as soon as possible, sprinkled with a little caster sugar. Continue until all the batter is used.

Serves 4.

Note: Mixing water with the milk helps to lighten pancake batter. Beer or cider can be used instead of milk.

CARIBBEAN CRÊPES

eight 17.5 cm (7 in) crêpes, see page 34	
4 bananas	
2 teaspoons lemon juice	
155 ml (5 fl oz/²⁄₃ cup) whipping cream	
30 g (1 oz/2 tablespoons) dark moist brown sugar	
½ teaspoon grated nutmeg	

Keep crêpes warm while preparing filling. Peel bananas and thinly slice one, then sprinkle with lemon juice and set aside. Whip cream to stiff peaks, and set aside about one-quarter for decoration.

Mash the remaining bananas and fold into cream with sugar and nutmeg. Divide mixture between crêpes and roll up firmly. Place on a serving dish and decorate with piped rosettes of cream and banana slices sprinkled with nutmeg.

Serves 4.

Variation: To make crêpes into mini cornets, cut each in half and roll into cornets. Carefully spoon the filling into the pockets, then decorate.

— FRENCH CHESTNUT CRÊPES —

eight 17.5 cm (7 in) crêpes, see page 34

250 g (8 oz) can sweetened chestnut purée

90 ml (3 fl oz/generous ⅓ cup) orange juice

3 teaspoons lemon juice

3 teaspoons white rum

30 g (1 oz/6 teaspoons) butter, melted

3 teaspoons icing sugar

Preheat oven to 150C (300F/Gas 2). Spread each crêpe with chestnut purée and fold into quarters. Place in a shallow flameproof dish. Mix together the orange juice, lemon juice and rum and pour over crêpes. Cover loosely with foil and heat through in the oven for 30 minutes.

Remove foil. Brush crêpes with butter and sprinkle with icing sugar, then put under a hot grill for 2 minutes, or until glazed. Serve at once.

Serves 4.

— CRÊPES SUZETTE —

eight 17.5 cm (7 in) crêpes, see page 34

90 g (3 oz/⅓ cup) unsalted butter

90 g (3 oz/½ cup) icing sugar

9 teaspoons orange juice

3 teaspoons lemon juice

6 teaspoons orange-flavoured liqueur

3 teaspoons brandy

orange slices and bay leaves, to garnish

Fold each crêpe in quarters. Put butter, icing sugar, orange juice and lemon juice into a large frying pan and heat gently until the butter has melted and the mixture is syrupy. Stir in the liqueur.

Put the crêpes in the pan and turn once so they are covered in sauce. Pour over the brandy and quickly light with a match. Serve as soon as the flames die down, garnished with orange slices and bay leaves.

Serves 4.

— MINCEMEAT CRÊPE GÂTEAU —

1 quantity of Basic Crêpes (see page 34)
357 g (12 oz) mincemeat (see Note)
1 eating apple
1 tablespoon brandy
grated peel of 1 orange
juice of ½ lemon
125 g (4 oz/1 cup) slivered almonds
4 tablespoons apricot jam, sieved

Make and cook pancakes as described on page 40. Preheat oven to 180C (350F/Gas 4). Put mincemeat into a saucepan. Peel, core and chop apple and add to pan.

Heat through, stirring from time to time, until apple is tender. Remove from heat and stir in brandy, orange peel, lemon juice and three-quarters of the almonds. Put a pancake on a greased ovenproof dish and spread with a little mincemeat mixture. Layer up gâteau, alternating pancakes and mincemeat, ending with a pancake.

Warm apricot jam in a small saucepan and pour over gâteau. Sprinkle with remaining almonds and place in oven for 15 minutes. Serve at once, cut in wedges, like a cake.

Serves 6.

Note: The mincemeat recipe on page 74 is not thick enough for this recipe. Use a good quality commercially prepared one.

— CHERRY & ALMOND LAYER —

eight 17.5 cm (7 in) crêpes, see page 34	
440 g (14 oz) can cherries	
90 g (3 oz/¼ cup) cherry jam	
3 teaspoons lemon juice	
60 g (2 oz/½ cup) ground almonds	
2 ripe eating pears, peeled and thinly sliced	
3 teaspoons icing sugar	

Keep crêpes warm while preparing filling. Drain cherries, reserving juice. Put jam into a small saucepan and warm over low heat until just runny, then stir in 6 teaspoons cherry juice and the lemon juice, almonds and pears. Remove from heat and stir in cherries.

Preheat oven to 160C (325F/Gas 3). Put one crêpe on a large ovenproof serving plate. Spread with some filling and top with a second crêpe. Repeat until all the crêpes and cherry mixture are used, finishing with a crêpe on the top. Heat through in the oven for 10 minutes, then sift icing sugar over the top and serve, cut into wedges.

Serves 4.

—— LEMON MERINGUE LAYER ——

eight 17.5 cm (7 in) crêpes, see page 34
1 quantity Fresh Lemon Topping, see page 37
2 egg whites
125 g (4 oz/½ cup) caster sugar
15 g (½ oz/2 tablespoons) whole blanched almonds
angelica 'leaves', to decorate

Keep crêpes warm while preparing lemon topping. Put one crêpe on a large ovenproof serving plate. Spread with some lemon topping. Top with a second crêpe and repeat until all the crêpes and the topping are used, finishing with a crêpe.

Preheat oven to 230C (450F/Gas 8). Whisk egg whites to stiff peaks, then fold in caster sugar. Cover top and sides of crêpes with meringue. Top with almonds and bake in the oven for 2 minutes, until pale golden. Decorate with angelica 'leaves', then serve at once, cut into wedges.

Serves 4.

—— BLACKBERRY APPLE STACK ——

eight 17.5 cm (7 in) crêpes, see page 34
500 g (1 lb) cooking apples
375 g (12 oz) blackberries
60 g (2 oz/¼ cup) sugar
2 egg whites
125 g (4 oz/½ cup) caster sugar

Keep crêpes warm while preparing filling. Peel, core and roughly chop the apples. Put into a saucepan with blackberries and sugar, and simmer over low heat until fruit is soft. Set aside for 10 minutes to cool.

Put one crêpe on large ovenproof serving plate and spread with some filling. Top with a second crêpe and repeat until all the crêpes and filling are used, finishing with a crêpe.

Preheat oven to 230C (450F/Gas 8). In a bowl, whisk egg whites to stiff peaks, then fold in caster sugar. Cover top and sides of crêpes with meringue and bake in the oven for 2 minutes, until pale golden. Serve at once, cut into wedges.

Serves 4.

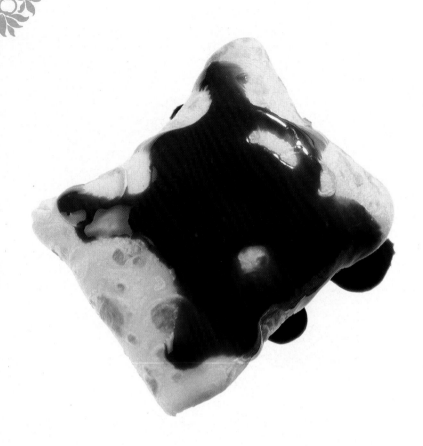

ICE CREAM CRÊPES

eight 17.5 cm (7 in) crêpes, see page 34
625 ml (20 fl oz) block vanilla ice cream
6 teaspoons cherry brandy
CHOCOLATE SAUCE
125 g (4 oz/½ cup) caster sugar
60 g (2oz/½ cup) cocoa

To make the chocolate sauce, put 155 ml (5 fl oz/⅔ cup) water and the sugar into a saucepan and stir over low heat until sugar has dissolved. Bring to boil, then simmer for 1 minute. Add cocoa and return to the boil, beating until smooth. Set aside and keep warm.

Cut ice cream into 8 cubes and wrap each one in a crêpe, then put two crêpes on to each plate. Sprinkle with cherry brandy and serve at once with hot chocolate sauce spooned over.

Serves 4.

CORNMEAL PANCAKES

60 g (2 oz/½ cup) cornmeal
315 ml (10 fl oz/1¼ cups) boiling water
315 ml (10 fl oz/1¼ cups) milk
250 g (8 oz/2 cups) plain flour
30 g (1 oz/6 teaspoons) granulated sugar
2 teaspoons baking powder
1 teaspoon salt
1 egg, beaten
30 g (1 oz/6 teaspoons) butter, melted
vegetable oil or lard for cooking
TO SERVE: butter and maple syrup

Put the cornmeal into a small saucepan. Add the boiling water and simmer for 5 minutes, stirring well. Transfer to a bowl and beat in the milk. In a separate bowl, stir together flour, sugar, baking powder and salt, then beat into the cornmeal mixture. Beat in the egg and butter.

Heat a heavy-based frying pan and lightly grease with vegetable oil or lard. Pour in batter to make 7.5 cm (3 in) rounds and cook until surface of each pancake is just set and covered with tiny bubbles. Turn with a palette knife and continue cooking on other side until golden. Remove from pan and serve warm with butter and maple syrup.

Makes 24.

BASIC WAFFLES

185 g (6 oz/1½ cups) plain flour
2 teaspoons baking powder
½ teaspoon salt
2 teaspoons sugar
2 eggs, separated
250 ml (8 fl oz/1 cup) milk
90 g (3 oz/⅓ cup) butter, melted
TO SERVE:
butter and maple syrup.

Sift flour, baking powder and salt into a bowl, then stir in sugar. Put egg yolks, milk and butter into a separate bowl and beat well, then add to dry ingredients. Beat hard to combine. Whisk egg whites in a bowl to stiff peaks and fold into the other ingredients.

Heat waffle iron, but do not grease. To test for correct heat, put 1 teaspoon water inside waffle iron, close and heat. When steaming stops, heat is correct.

Put 3 teaspoons batter into centre of each compartment, close and cook until puffed up and golden brown. Lift out waffles with a fork, set aside and keep warm, then continue until all the batter is used. Serve hot with butter and maple syrup.

Makes 6.

Variation: Serve the waffles sandwiched together with whipped cream. Decorate with soft fruit and icing sugar.

BANANA NUT WAFFLES

185 g (6 oz/1½ cups) plain flour
2 teaspoons baking powder
½ teaspoon salt
2 teaspoons sugar
2 eggs, separated
250 ml (8 fl oz/1 cup) milk
90 g (3 oz/½ cup) butter, melted
90 g (3 oz/¾ cup) walnuts, finely chopped
2 bananas
30 g (1 oz/2 tablespoons) icing sugar
3 teaspoons lemon juice

Sift flour, baking powder and salt into a bowl, then stir in sugar. Put egg yolks, milk and butter into a bowl and beat well, then add to dry ingredients and beat hard to combine. Stir in 3 teaspoons of the chopped walnuts.

Whisk egg whites in a bowl to stiff peaks and fold into other ingredients.

Heat waffle iron, but do not grease. Put 3 teaspoons batter into centre of each compartment, close and cook until puffed up and golden brown. Lift out waffles with a fork, set aside and keep warm in a low oven, then continue until all the batter is used.

While waffles are cooking, peel and slice bananas into a bowl with icing sugar and lemon juice. Serve the hot waffles topped with banana slices and sprinkle over remaining walnuts.

Makes 6.

— STRAWBERRY RUM WAFFLES —

6 Basic Waffles, see page 43

250 g (8 oz) strawberries, hulled and thickly sliced

60 g (2 oz/¼ cup) caster sugar

6 teaspoons white rum

6 scoops strawberry ice cream

While the waffles are cooking, prepare the topping. Put the strawberries into a bowl with the sugar and rum, stir well and leave to stand until waffles are ready.

Spoon strawberries and their soaking liquid over hot waffles, then top each one with a scoop of ice cream. Serve at once.

Serves 6.

Note: Orange juice makes an excellent substitute for the rum, if desired.

— CHOCOLATE CREAM WAFFLES —

185 g (6 oz/1½ cups) plain flour

2 teaspoons baking powder

½ teaspoon salt

30 g (1 oz/6 teaspoons) sugar

60 g (2 oz) plain (dark) chocolate

2 eggs, separated

250 ml (8 fl oz/1 cup) milk

90 g (3 oz/⅓ cup) butter, melted

few drops vanilla essence

TO SERVE:

155 ml (5 fl oz/⅔ cup) whipping cream

grated chocolate

Sift flour, baking powder and salt into a bowl, then stir in sugar. Melt chocolate in the top of a double boiler or a bowl set over a saucepan of simmering water.

Put egg yolks, milk, butter and chocolate into a bowl with the vanilla essence and beat well. Add to dry ingredients and beat hard to combine. Whisk egg whites in a bowl to stiff peaks and fold into other ingredients.

Heat waffle iron, but do not grease. Put 3 teaspoons batter into centre of each compartment. Close and cook until puffed up and crisp. Lift out waffles with a fork, set aside and keep warm, then continue until all the batter is used. Whip cream to soft peaks in a bowl. Serve hot waffles with cream piped on top or in bowl for spooning over. Decorate with grated chocolate.

Makes 6.

FRUIT DESSERTS

FRUIT FRITTERS

4 cooking or crisp tart eating apples
2-3 tablespoons calvados or cognac
3 tablespoons caster sugar
125 g (4 oz/1 cup) plain flour
pinch of salt
2 eggs, separated
155 ml (5 fl oz/²⁄₃ cup) milk
1 tablespoon oil
oil for deep frying
icing sugar

Peel, core and cut apples into rings.

In a shallow dish, mix calvados or cognac with half the sugar. Add apples, turning them over to coat. Leave to macerate for 30 minutes. Sift flour and salt into a large bowl and mix in remaining sugar. Make a well in centre and drop in egg yolks. Using a wooden spoon, draw flour into yolks while gradually adding milk. Beat to a smooth batter, then leave to stand for 30 minutes. In a separate bowl, whisk egg whites until stiff and fold into batter with 1 tablespoon oil.

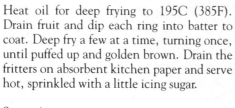

Heat oil for deep frying to 195C (385F). Drain fruit and dip each ring into batter to coat. Deep fry a few at a time, turning once, until puffed up and golden brown. Drain the fritters on absorbent kitchen paper and serve hot, sprinkled with a little icing sugar.

Serves 4.

Variations: Use pineapple, pears or bananas in place of apples, soaking them in an appropriate liqueur for 30 minutes.

CARAMEL FRUIT KEBABS

selection of fruit, such as 2 bananas, 2 pears, 1 small
   pineapple, 2 peaches, grapes and strawberries
60 g (2 oz/¼ cup) butter, melted
2 tablespoons caster sugar
Mousseline Sauce (see page 90), to serve, if desired

MARINADE: 1 tablespoon lemon juice
3 tablespoons brandy
1-2 tablespoons clear honey
125 ml (4 fl oz/½ cup) orange juice
cinnamon stick, broken into pieces

In a large bowl, mix together all the ingredients for the marinade.

To prepare fruit, cut bananas into 2.5 cm (1 in) pieces, peel and core pears and cut in chunks, cut pineapple into thick slices then peel and discard core and cut flesh in chunks, skin peaches and cut flesh in chunks, leave grapes whole. Add these to the marinade and stir very gently to coat evenly, then leave for 2 hours. Add whole strawberries to marinade 15 minutes before end of marinating time.

Drain fruit, reserving marinade. Thread fruit onto 6 kebab sticks, brush with melted butter and sprinkle with sugar. Place under a medium grill for 7-8 minutes, turning frequently. Brush with any leftover butter and sprinkle with remaining sugar while turning. Strain marinade into a saucepan and heat gently. Serve with the kebabs with Mousseline Sauce, if using.

Serves 6.

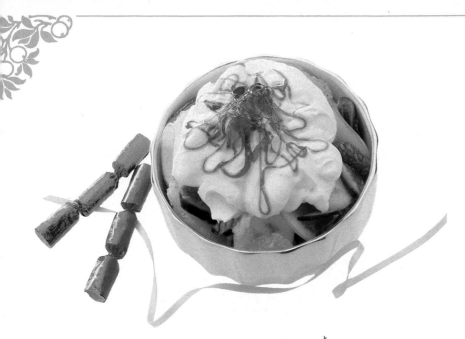

FROSTIE FRUIT BRULÉES

2 oranges
2 eating apples
2 figs
2 bananas, sliced
125 g (4 oz) grapes, seeded
6 teaspoons Marsala
625 ml (20 fl oz/2½ cups) double (thick) cream
185 g (6 oz/¾ cup) caster sugar
60 ml (2 fl oz/¼ cup) boiling water

Using a sharp knife, cut orange peel and pith away from flesh. Cut between membranes to remove segments. Quarter and core apples; slice thinly. Cut figs into thin wedges.

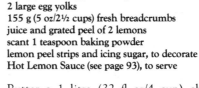

Mix all the fruit gently together in a bowl with Marsala. Divide fruit between 6 individual dishes. Place cream in a bowl and whip until very thick. Spoon cream evenly over the fruit. Chill until ready to serve.

Place sugar and water in a saucepan and heat gently, stirring occasionally, until sugar has dissolved. Boil rapidly until syrup turns a golden brown colour. Allow bubbles to subside, then drizzle caramel over top of fruit and cream. Serve immediately.

Serves 6.

LEMON BELVOIR PUDDING

125 g (4 oz/½ cup) butter, softened
125 g (4 oz/½ cup) caster sugar
2 large egg yolks
155 g (5 oz/2½ cups) fresh breadcrumbs
juice and grated peel of 2 lemons
scant 1 teaspoon baking powder
lemon peel strips and icing sugar, to decorate
Hot Lemon Sauce (see page 93), to serve

Butter a 1 litre (32 fl oz/4 cup) charlotte mould thoroughly. In a large bowl, cream butter and sugar until light and fluffy.

Beat in egg yolks and breadcrumbs. When well mixed, stir in lemon juice and grated peel and baking powder. Spoon into prepared mould and cover top with a piece of foil, pleated in the middle. Tie securely with string round mould, then place in a saucepan with enough gently boiling water to come halfway up sides.

Steam for 45-60 minutes. Check water in pan from time to time and add more boiling water as necessary. Turn out pudding and decorate with strips of lemon peel. Dust with icing sugar and serve hot with Hot Lemon Sauce.

Serves 4.

APPLE CHARLOTTE

750 g (1½ lb) eating apples
grated peel of 1 lemon
90 g (3 oz/½ cup) brown sugar
125 g (4 oz/½ cup) butter
155 g (5 oz/2½ cups) coarse fresh breadcrumbs
apple slices and mint sprigs, to decorate

Peel, core and slice apples. Put into a saucepan with grated lemon peel, 60 g (2 oz/⅓ cup) of the sugar and 30 g (1 oz/6 teaspoons) of the butter. Simmer, covered, over a low heat until soft. Beat until pulpy.

Melt remaining butter in a frying pan and fry breadcrumbs until golden brown, stirring constantly to prevent burning. Stir in remaining sugar and leave to cool.

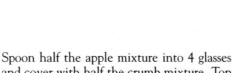

Spoon half the apple mixture into 4 glasses and cover with half the crumb mixture. Top with remaining apple and crumbs. Chill in the refrigerator for 2 hours before serving. Decorate with apple slices and sprigs of mint.

Serves 4.

BAKED DEMELZA APPLES

60 g (2 oz/⅓ cup) mixed raisins and sultanas
5 tablespoons ginger wine, Madeira or sweet sherry
4 large cooking apples
90 g (3 oz/¾ cup) toasted, flaked almonds
1-2 tablespoons marmalade
chilled whipped cream, to serve

Preheat oven to 180C (350F/Gas 4). Put raisins and sultanas into a small bowl and add ginger wine, Madeira or sherry. Leave to soak for several hours.

Wash and dry apples, but do not peel. Remove core using an apple corer and score a line around each apple. Stand the apples in an ovenproof dish. Drain dried fruit, reserving liquid. Mix fruit with almonds and marmalade in a bowl, then fill the apple cavities with this mixture, pushing it down firmly. Pour strained liquid over apples.

Bake the apples in the oven for 45-60 minutes, until soft. Pile a spoonful of whipped cream on top of each apple and serve immediately.

Serves 4.

SPOTTED DICK

CHERRY CLAFOUTI

125 g (4 oz/1 cup) self-raising flour
9 teaspoons cornflour
1 teaspoon baking powder
125 g (4 oz/½ cup) caster sugar
125 g (4 oz/½ cup) butter, softened
juice and grated peel of 1 orange
2 eggs
125 g (4 oz/¾ cup) sultanas
60 g (2 oz/⅓ cup) chopped mixed citrus peel
Mousseline Sauce (see page 90) or Blackcurrant
  Sauce (see page 90), to serve

Butter a 940 ml (30 fl oz/3¾ cup) pudding
bowl or a 20 cm (8 in) ring mould. Sift flour,
cornflour and baking powder onto a plate.

In a large bowl, cream sugar, butter and grated
orange peel until light and fluffy. In a separate
bowl, beat eggs with orange juice, then beat
this gradually into butter mixture with 1
tablespoon flour mixture. Fold in remaining
flour with sultanas and citrus peel. The
mixture should be a soft, dropping
consistency (if it is too stiff, add a little milk).

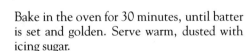

Spoon mixture into prepared bowl or mould
and cover top with a piece of buttered foil,
pleated in middle. Tie securely with string
round rim of bowl or mould and place in
saucepan of gently boiling water to come
halfway up sides. Steam for 1½-2 hours. Turn
out and serve warm with Mousseline Sauce or
Blackcurrant Sauce.

Serves 6.

Note: Wash fruit before using in a pudding or
cake to remove the coating of oil or sugar.

750 g (1½ lb) stoned black cherries, fresh or frozen,
  thawed if frozen
90 g (3 oz/¾ cup) plain flour
pinch of salt
3 eggs
90 g (3 oz/⅓ cup) caster sugar
500 ml (16 fl oz/2 cups) milk
1 tablespoon cherry brandy or kirsch
icing sugar, to serve

Preheat oven to 200C (400F/Gas 6). Drain
the cherries, if thawed. Butter a 1.25 litre
(40 fl oz/5 cup) pie dish and put cherries in it.

Sift flour and salt together onto a plate. In a
large bowl, beat eggs with sugar until creamy,
then fold in flour. Warm milk slightly in a
saucepan over a low heat and stir into egg
mixture with cherry brandy or kirsch. Beat
well to make batter smooth, then pour the
batter over the cherries.

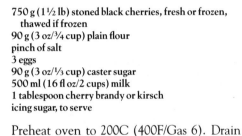

Bake in the oven for 30 minutes, until batter
is set and golden. Serve warm, dusted with
icing sugar.

Serves 6.

Note: Fresh cherries can taste a little bland
when cooked. Add 1-2 drops almond essence
to improve the flavour, if desired.

ROUND CHRISTMAS PUDDING

TIPSY FRUIT JELLY

500 g (1 lb/3 cups) mixed dried fruit
60 g (2 oz/½ cup) chopped prunes
45 g (1½ oz/⅓ cup) chopped glacé cherries
60 g (2 oz/½ cup) chopped almonds
45 g (1½ oz/¼ cup) grated carrot
45 g (1½ oz/¼ cup) grated cooking apple
finely grated peel and juice of 1 orange
3 teaspoons black treacle (molasses)
90 ml (3 fl oz/⅓ cup) stout
3 teaspoons brandy plus extra for serving
1 egg
60 g (2 oz/¼ cup) butter, melted
60 g (2 oz/⅓ cup) dark soft brown sugar
¾ teaspoon ground allspice
60 g (2 oz/½ cup) plain flour
60 g (2 oz/1 cup) soft white breadcrumbs

3 lemons
125 g (4 oz/½ cup) caster sugar
155 ml (5 fl oz/⅔ cup) claret
22 g (¾ oz/6 teaspoons) powdered gelatine
12 teaspoons hot water
375 g (12 oz) mixed fruit (grapes, lychees, pineapple
 and clementines)
whipped cream, to decorate

Using a potato peeler or sharp knife, pare the peel from lemons; squeeze out juice. Place peel in a saucepan with 315 ml (10 fl oz/1¼ cups) water and bring to boil. Add sugar; stir until dissolved.

In a large mixing bowl, put mixed fruit, prunes, cherries, almonds, carrot, apple, orange peel and juice, treacle, stout and the brandy. Mix well together. Stir in egg, butter, sugar, allspice, flour and breadcrumbs until well blended. Cover; leave in a cool place until ready to cook. Use a buttered round Christmas pudding mould, measuring 12.5 cm (5 in) in diameter, or a rice steaming mould, lined with double thickness foil. Fill each half of mould with mixture. Place two halves together, securing mould tightly.

Leave the mixture until cold, then strain into a measuring jug; stir in the lemon juice. Pour ⅓ lemon mixture into a bowl, add claret and stir until blended. Sprinkle gelatine over hot water in a small bowl; leave to soften. Stand bowl in a saucepan of hot water, stir until dissolved and quite hot. Add ½ gelatine to claret mixture, stirring well, and the remainder to lemon mixture, stirring well. Halve grapes and lychees, remove seeds and stones. Peel and slice pineapple and clementines.

Half-fill a saucepan with water, bring to the boil and place mould carefully into pan so that water comes just below join of mould. Cover and cook very gently for 6 hours. Cool in mould; turn out and wrap in foil until required. To re-heat pudding: unwrap and replace in mould. Cook as before for 2-3 hours. Turn onto a serving plate, decorate with holly, spoon over warmed brandy and set alight. Serve with Brandy Butter, see page 95.

Serves 8.

Arrange ¼ of mixed fruit in base of 6 individual moulds or glasses. Spoon enough lemon jelly over fruit to cover. Leave to set. Arrange a second layer of fruit over set jelly layer and cover with claret jelly; leave to set. Repeat to make another lemon fruit layer and claret fruit layer. When jelly has set firm, turn out of moulds by dipping quickly into hand-hot water and inverting onto a plate, or serve in glasses, if preferred. Decorate with whipped cream.

Makes 6.

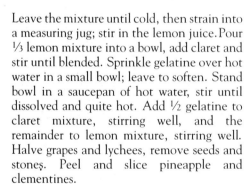

KISSEL

750 g (1½ lb) canned or bottled blackcurrants
250 g (8 oz) canned or bottled stoned black cherries
1 tablespoon arrowroot
juice and grated peel of 1 orange
250 g (8 oz) fresh raspberries
2 tablespoons crème de cassis
Meringues (see page 30) or shortbread biscuits, to serve, if desired

Drain blackcurrants and cherries, reserving 500 ml (16 fl oz/2 cups) juice. Put the juice into a saucepan and bring to the boil.

In a small bowl, mix arrowroot with orange juice and add to juices in pan with orange peel. Stir over medium heat until juices are thick and clear; the syrup should boil for 1-2 minutes to cook the arrowroot.

Place blackcurrants, cherries and raspberries in a glass serving dish. Pour thickened juices over them and cool. Stir in cassis. Chill in the refrigerator. Serve with meringues or shortbread biscuits, if desired.

Serves 6.

Note: Add liqueur to this dish when the syrup is cold. This way the flavour of the liqueur remains unaltered.

KUMQUATS IN COGNAC

500 g (1 lb) kumquats
375 g (12 oz/1½ cups) granulated sugar
155 ml (5 fl oz/⅔ cup) cognac

Have ready 2 or 3 small, clean, dry, warm sterilised glass jars with well-fitting lids. Remove stalks and wash kumquats thoroughly; dry on absorbent kitchen paper. Place 315 ml (10 fl oz/1¼ cups) water in a medium-sized saucepan, add 125 g (4 oz/½ cup) sugar and heat gently, stirring occasionally, until sugar has dissolved.

Bring to boil, add kumquats and cook very gently for 2-3 minutes, taking care kumquats do not split open. Remove kumquats with a slotted spoon and place on a plate. Reserve syrup. Place kumquats carefully in jars without packing them too tightly, so they come to neck of jar. Measure 155 ml (5 fl oz/⅔ cup) of remaining syrup and put in a saucepan with remaining sugar. Stir over a gentle heat until sugar has dissolved.

Boil rapidly for 1 minute until syrupy. Test by placing a drop of syrup between 2 cold teaspoons: press together, then pull apart – a fine thread of sugar should form. Pour sugar syrup into measuring jug and add the same amount of cognac. Stir well and fill each jar to the brim with cognac syrup. Seal jars with well-fitting lids, label and store in a cool place for up to 3 months.

Makes 2-3 jars.

FRUIT DUFF

375 g (12 oz) mixed fresh or frozen fruit,
  blackcurrants, plums or gooseberries, thawed if
  frozen
125 g (4 oz/½ cup) caster sugar
185 g (6oz/1½ cups) self-raising flour
2 teaspoons baking powder
pinch of salt
15 g (½ oz/3 teaspoons) butter
about 75 ml (2½ fl oz/⅓ cup) milk
Crème à Vanille (see page 91) or Mousseline Sauce
  (see page 90), to serve

Drain the fruit, if thawed. Grease a 1.25 litre
(40 fl oz/5 cup) pudding bowl and put the
mixed fruit into it.

Add half the sugar to fruit (add a little more if
using tart fruit such as gooseberries). Sift
flour, baking powder and salt into a large bowl
and stir in remaining sugar. Rub in butter
with fingertips until incorporated into dry
ingredients. Add milk and stir to form a soft
dough. Turn out onto a lightly floured
surface, and pat to a circle to fit top of
pudding bowl. Place on top of fruit.

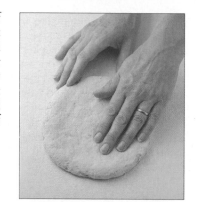

Cover bowl with a piece of foil, pleated in
middle. Tie securely with string round rim of
bowl. Place in saucepan of gently boiling
water to come halfway up sides and steam for
1½ hours. Check water in pan from time to
time and add more boiling water as necessary.
Turn out and serve hot, with Crème à la
Vanille or Mousseline Sauce.

Serves 4.

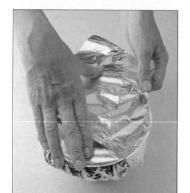

PEARS IN WINE

2 eating pears
315 ml (10 fl oz/1¼ cups) sweet dessert wine, such as
  Beaume de Venise, or red wine
½ orange
½ lemon
60 g (2 oz/¼ cup) caster sugar
cream, to serve

Peal pears with a vegetable peeler, leaving
stalks intact. Cut out as much core as possible
from 'flower' end, then lay on their sides in a
small saucepan: they should fit snugly. Cover
with dessert wine.

Peel off as much peel as possible from the
orange and lemon halves, using a canelle
knife. Alternatively, use a vegetable peeler
and peel thinly so as to get no pith, then cut
peel into julienne strips. Squeeze juice from
orange and lemon halves and add to pan with
peel strips and sugar. Cover and poach pears
on a low heat until just tender.

Remove with slotted spoon to a bowl. Pour
over cooking liquid and leave to cool, then
chill for 2 hours. Boil the cooking liquid
vigorously until syrupy and reduced by half.
Pour the syrup over the pears just before
serving. Serve with the cream.

Serves 2.

Note: If you have wine left over from cooking
or a meal, pour it over dried fruit and keep in a
screw-top jar. The fruit will plump up and
gives a lovely flavour to fruit cakes.

SUMMER PUDDING

500 g (1 lb) redcurrants and blackcurrants, mixed
juice of ½ orange
125 g (4 oz/½ cup) caster sugar
250 g (8 oz) raspberries
12-16 slices thin white bread
extra raspberries, if desired, and whipping cream, to
  serve

Put currants into a saucepan with orange juice and sugar and cook over a low heat, stirring occasionally, until juicy and just tender. Gently stir in raspberries, then set aside to cool.

Cut crusts from bread. From 6 slices, cut circles the same size as the top of small ramekin dishes or dariole moulds. Use remaining bread to line 6 ramekin dishes or dariole moulds, overlapping bread to line dishes completely. Strain fruit, reserving juices, and spoon fruit into bread-lined dishes, pressing down quite firmly. Cover with bread circles. Pour some of the reserved juice into dishes to soak bread. Put a small weight on top of each pudding.

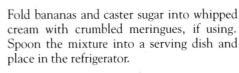

Chill puddings and remaining juice, for several hours or overnight. When ready to serve, turn puddings out onto individual plates and spoon a little of the reserved juices around them. Top with the extra raspberries, if desired. Whip cream lightly and dot a small amount in the juice and serve the remaining cream separately.

Serves 6.

BANANA BRÛLÉE

625 ml (20 fl oz/2½ cups) whipping cream
3 large bananas
juice of 1 small lemon
60 g (2 oz/¼ cup) caster sugar
few crumbled meringues (see page 30), if desired
125 g (4 oz/½ cup) granulated sugar

In a large bowl, whip cream until thick. Slice bananas thinly into a separate bowl and toss in lemon juice.

Fold bananas and caster sugar into whipped cream with crumbled meringues, if using. Spoon the mixture into a serving dish and place in the refrigerator.

Put granulated sugar and 1 tablespoon water into a small saucepan and place over a low heat to dissolve sugar. Do not stir. When sugar has dissolved, increase heat and boil syrup to a rich brown caramel. Immediately dribble this over banana cream mixture, then replace in refrigerator for caramel to harden. Serve within 1-2 hours.

Serves 6.

FLAMING FRUIT SALAD

TROPICAL FRUIT COCKTAIL

500 g (1 lb/7½ cups) mixed dried fruit, such as prunes, apricots, figs, apples, pears and peaches
2 tablespoons sherry
juice of ½ lemon
2 tablespoons clear honey
½ cinnamon stick
4 tablespoons brandy
90 g (3 oz/¾ cup) toasted almond flakes
60 g (2 oz/½ cup) walnuts, coarsely chopped
chilled single (light) cream or ice cream, to serve

Soak fruit overnight in 625 ml (20 fl oz/2½ cups) water and the sherry.

juice of 2 oranges
selection of tropical fruits, such as 2 mangoes
2 nectarines, 3 kiwi fruit, 4 passion fruit,
1 pineapple, 1 small ogen melon

MANGO CREAM: 1 large ripe mango
juice of ½ orange
1 tablespoon kirsch, if desired
squeeze of lemon juice
1 tablespoon caster sugar
250 ml (8 fl oz/1 cup) whipping cream

Strain the orange juice into a jug.

Put fruit and soaking liquid into a saucepan with lemon juice, honey and cinnamon stick. Cover and simmer on a low heat until fruit is just tender. Discard cinnamon stick, transfer fruit to serving dish and keep warm.

To prepare fruit, peel mangoes, discard stone and slice flesh evenly. Cut nectarines in half, remove stone and slice flesh evenly. Peel kiwi fruit and slice crosswise thinly. Cut passion fruit, but leave flesh in shells. Cut pineapple in half, discard leaves or use to decorate serving plate, then peel, core and slice flesh into chunks. Cut melon in half, discard seeds and scoop out flesh using a melon baller, or slice it. Arrange fruit in rows on a large serving plate.

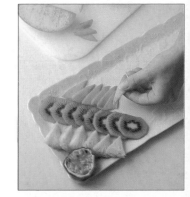

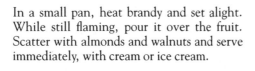

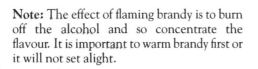

In a small pan, heat brandy and set alight. While still flaming, pour it over the fruit. Scatter with almonds and walnuts and serve immediately, with cream or ice cream.

Serves 5-6.

Note: The effect of flaming brandy is to burn off the alcohol and so concentrate the flavour. It is important to warm brandy first or it will not set alight.

Sprinkle fruit with the strained orange juice, cover with plastic wrap and chill until ready to serve. To make mango cream, peel mango, discard stone and purée flesh in a blender or food processor with orange juice, kirsch, if using, and lemon juice. Fold in sugar. In a bowl, whip cream stiffly, then fold in the purée, to make cream streaky, using a knife to give a marbled effect. Chill until required. Serve in a glass bowl with fruit platter.

Serves 6.

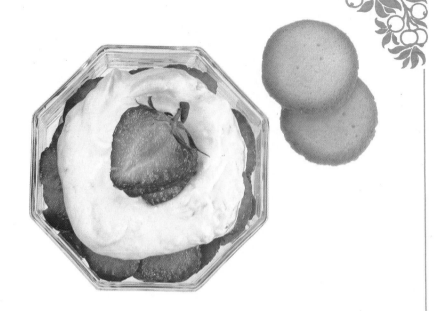

LIME & TANGERINE GÂTEAU

12 trifle sponges
155 ml (5 fl oz/²/₃ cup) double (thick) cream
9 teaspoons fromage frais
25 g (1 oz/¼ cup) chopped pistachio nuts
lime and tangerine wedges, to decorate

FILLING: 3 eggs, separated
250 g (8 oz/1 cup) curd cheese
125 g (4 oz/½ cup) caster sugar
finely grated peel and juice of 2 tangerines
finely grated peel and juice of 2 limes
5 teaspoons powdered gelatine

To make filling, put egg yolks, curd cheese
and sugar in a bowl. Beat until smooth.

Stir in fruit peels and ½ of juices. Sprinkle
gelatine over 9 teaspoons water in a bowl;
leave to soften. Stand bowl in a pan of hot
water; stir until dissolved. Stir into cheese
mixture; leave until thick. Line a 17.5 cm (7
in) square tin with plastic wrap. Cut sponges
into 3 thin layers; line base and sides of tin.
Sprinkle with ⅓ of remaining fruit juice.
Stiffly whisk egg whites; fold into cheese
mixture. Pour ½ into tin, cover with a layer
of sponge; sprinkle with ⅓ juice.

Top with remaining sponge and juice. Cover
with plastic wrap and chill until set. Turn
gâteau onto a serving plate; remove plastic
wrap. Whip cream and fromage frais until
thick, place ¼ in a piping bag fitted with a
small star nozzle. Spread remaining cream
over gâteau; press pistachio nuts onto sides.
Pipe a border around top and base of gâteau.
Decorate with lime and tangerine wedges.

Serves 12.

STRAWBERRIES ROMANOFF

750 g (1½ lb) fresh strawberries, hulled
grated peel of 1 orange
4 teaspoons Grand Marnier
315 ml (10 fl oz/1¼ cups) whipping cream
2 tablespoons crème fraîche
1-2 tablespoons icing sugar
langues de chat or round biscuits, to serve

Reserve 4 strawberries for decoration and
slice the remainder into a bowl. Add orange
peel and Grand Marnier, gently mix together,
then leave to macerate for 15 minutes.

In a bowl, whip the cream until quite stiff and
fold in the crème fraîche. Sift icing sugar over
cream and fold in. Put a spoonful of
macerated strawberries into 4 glasses. Mash
the remaining strawberries gently and fold
into the whipped cream mixture.

Carefully spoon the mixture over the
strawberries in the glasses and chill in the
refrigerator until ready to serve. Decorate
each glass with one of the reserved
strawberries cut into a fan shape. Serve with
langues de chat or round biscuits.

Serves 4.

Note: Do not hull strawberries until ready to
use them.

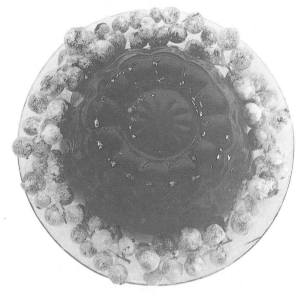

TART LEMON MOULD

625 ml (20 fl oz/2½ cups) milk
90 g (3 oz/⅓ cup) granulated sugar
3 teaspoons powdered gelatine
3 small egg yolks
grated peel and juice of 1 large lemon
90 g (3 oz/⅓ cup) caster sugar
lemon twists and herb sprigs, to decorate

Put milk, granulated sugar and gelatine into a small saucepan and set over a low heat. Bring almost to boiling point (but do not boil), stirring constantly. Remove from heat.

In a bowl, beat egg yolks together lightly and gradually pour hot milk over them, stirring all the time. Pour into a 940 ml (30 fl oz/3¾ cup) mould. Leave at room temperature until cold, then refrigerate until set.

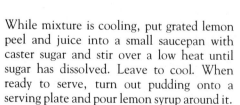

While mixture is cooling, put grated lemon peel and juice into a small saucepan with caster sugar and stir over a low heat until sugar has dissolved. Leave to cool. When ready to serve, turn out pudding onto a serving plate and pour lemon syrup around it. Decorate with lemon twists and herbs.

Serves 4.

PORT JELLY

625 ml (20 fl oz/2½ cups) ruby port
peel and juice of ½ orange
peel and juice of 1 lemon
90 g (3 oz/⅓ cup) caster sugar
1 cinnamon stick
5 teaspoons powdered gelatine

FROSTED FRUIT: 1 egg white
small bunches redcurrants and/or seedless grapes
caster sugar

Put port into a saucepan. Using a vegetable peeler, peel the orange half and the lemon thinly and add to port with lemon juice and squeezed lemon shell.

Add sugar and cinnamon stick and heat gently until sugar has dissolved. Leave to infuse for 20 minutes. Sprinkle gelatine on to squeezed orange juice in a small bowl and leave to soften for 2-3 minutes. Stand bowl in a saucepan of hot water and stir until gelatine has dissolved. Stir into port, then strain the mixture through a fine sieve into a wetted 815 ml (26 fl oz/3¼ cup) mould.

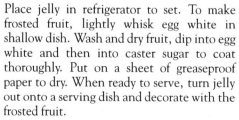

Place jelly in refrigerator to set. To make frosted fruit, lightly whisk egg white in shallow dish. Wash and dry fruit, dip into egg white and then into caster sugar to coat thoroughly. Put on a sheet of greaseproof paper to dry. When ready to serve, turn jelly out onto a serving dish and decorate with the frosted fruit.

Serves 4-6.

CHOCOLATE DESSERTS

NEGRESSE EN CHEMISE

185 g (6 oz) plain (dark) chocolate
5 tablespoons strong black coffee
185 g (6 oz/¾ cup) unsalted butter
185 g (6 oz/¾ cup) caster sugar
5 large eggs, beaten
375 ml (12 fl oz/1½ cups) whipping cream

Preheat oven to 180C (350F/Gas 4). Line a 1 litre (32 fl oz/4 cup) pudding bowl or soufflé dish with double thickness of foil.

Melt chocolate with coffee in top of a double boiler or a bowl set over a saucepan of simmering water. Gradually beat in butter and sugar and heat until mixture is hot. Remove from heat and gradually whisk in eggs. Strain mixture into prepared dish, cover with foil and place in a roasting tin. Add boiling water to tin to come halfway up dish, then bake in the oven for 65 minutes, until top has a thick crust. Cool, then refrigerate.

When ready to serve, unmould pudding onto a serving dish and peel away foil – you need to do this carefully as the pudding is rich and sticky. In a bowl, whip cream stiffly, then cover the cake with two-thirds of it. Use remainder to pipe cream rosettes round top edge and base of cake.

Serves 6-8.

Note: The pudding looks very pretty decorated with tiny sprigs of fresh flowers.

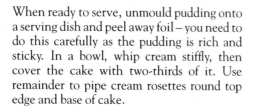

CHOCOLATE TRIFLE

100 g (3½ oz) plain (dark) chocolate
4 tablespoons rum and water, mixed
4 egg yolks
1 tablespoon caster sugar
750 ml (24 fl oz/3 cups) whipping cream
250 g (8 oz) plain or trifle sponge cakes
185 g (6 oz/½ cup) apricot jam
375 g (12 oz) mixed fruit, such as grapes, ripe pears and bananas
grated chocolate, to decorate

Melt chocolate with rum and water in a double boiler or a bowl set over a saucepan of simmering water. Set over medium heat and stir until smooth.

In a large bowl, whisk egg yolks and sugar together until light and fluffy. Put 315 ml (10 fl oz/1¼ cups) cream into a pan and bring almost to boiling point. Whisk into yolk mixture with chocolate. Return mixture to saucepan and whisk over a very low heat until chocolate is incorporated and mixture has thickened slightly. Slice sponges in half. Warm jam slightly in a small saucepan, then brush over the sponges.

Place sponges in a glass serving bowl or individual glass dishes. To prepare fruit, halve and seed grapes, peel, core and finely slice pears and slice bananas. Scatter fruit over sponges. Lightly whip remaining cream, then spoon chocolate sauce over fruit and spread half the cream over it. Continue whisking remaining cream to stiff peaks and use to decorate, then sprinkle with grated chocolate. Chill in the refrigerator until ready to serve.

Serves 6.

CHOCOLATE PEARS

60 g (2 oz) Amaretti biscuits
3-4 tablespoons Cointreau
125 g (4 oz) plain (dark) chocolate
3 tablespoons strong black coffee
1 tablespoon orange juice
30 g (1 oz/6 teaspoons) butter
2 eggs, separated
4 ripe pears

Put Amaretti biscuits into a bowl, pour over liqueur, then crush biscuits to rough crumbs using end of rolling pin.

Melt chocolate with coffee and orange juice in the top of a double boiler or a bowl set over a saucepan of simmering water. When smooth, remove from heat and beat in butter and egg yolks. In a separate bowl, whisk egg whites until stiff and fold chocolate mixture into them. Set aside. Peel pears, leaving them whole with stalks intact. Hollow out as much core as possible from the base and fill cavity with crumb mixture.

Stand the pears on a plate, cutting off a small slice if necessary to make them stand upright. Spoon chocolate mixture over pears to coat evenly. Chill for several hours or overnight. Transfer to individual plates using a fish slice when ready to serve.

Serves 4.

RICH CHOCOLATE LOG

440 g (14 oz) can condensed milk
90 g (3 oz) plain (dark) chocolate
45 g (1½ oz/9 teaspoons) butter
500 g (1 lb) plain sponge cake
125 g (4 oz/⅔ cup) glacé cherries, halved
45 g (1½ oz/½ cup) walnuts, chopped
45 g (1½ oz/3 tablespoons) stoned dates, chopped

CHOCOLATE FUDGE ICING: 45 g (1½ oz/9 teaspoons) butter
60 g (2 oz/¼ cup) caster sugar
90 g (3 oz/½ cup) icing sugar
30 g (1 oz/¼ cup) cocoa

Put milk, chocolate and butter in a saucepan and stir over low heat until chocolate and butter have melted and ingredients are well combined. Remove from heat. Reduce cake to crumbs in a blender or food processor and stir into chocolate mixture. Stir in the cherries, walnuts and dates. Spoon mixture onto a large piece of greaseproof paper and form into a log shape. Roll up in the paper and chill overnight.

Two hours before serving, unwrap roll and place on serving dish. To make the fudge icing, melt the butter in a saucepan with caster sugar and 2 tablespoons water. Bring to boiling point. Sift icing sugar and cocoa into pan and beat well. Cool until fudgy, then spread over roll. Mark lines along roll with a fork to give a log effect.

Serves 8-10.

GÂTEAU GRENOBLE

CHOC CHESTNUT GÂTEAU

60 g (2 oz/¹⁄₃ cup) hazelnuts, skinned
4 eggs, separated, plus 1 extra white
140 g (4¹⁄₂ oz/¹⁄₂ cup plus 3 teaspoons) caster sugar
90 g (3 oz) plain (dark) chocolate
250 g (8 oz/2¹⁄₂ cups) walnuts, finely chopped
155 ml (5 fl oz/²⁄₃ cup) whipping cream

Preheat oven to 150C (300F/Gas 2). Butter a 1 kg (2 lb) loaf tin very well. Grind hazelnuts in a coffee grinder or food processor. In a large bowl, beat egg yolks together, then gradually beat in all but 3 teaspoons of the sugar, until mixture is light and fluffy.

185 g (6 oz/³⁄₄ cup) butter, softened
125 g (4 oz/¹⁄₂ cup) caster sugar
185 g (6 oz) plain (dark) chocolate
3 tablespoons strong black coffee
440 g (14 oz) can unsweetened chestnut purée
315 ml (10 fl oz/1¹⁄₄ cups) whipping cream
marrons glacés, to decorate, if desired

Oil a loose-bottomed or springform 20 cm (8 in) round or 1 kg (2 lb) loaf tin. Cream butter and sugar in a bowl until they are light and fluffy.

Melt chocolate in top of a double boiler or bowl set over a saucepan of simmering water, then stir into yolk mixture with hazelnuts and walnuts. In a large bowl, whisk egg whites until stiff, but not dry. Sprinkle in remaining sugar and whisk again until mixture is glossy. Fold 2-3 tablespoons into chocolate mixture.

Melt chocolate with coffee in top of a double boiler or bowl set over a saucepan of simmering water. Add chestnut purée to butter mixture with melted chocolate and beat until smooth. Spoon mixture into prepared tin and level surface. Cover with foil and freeze for 3 hours.

Carefully fold remaining egg white into mixture – this is quite hard to do as chocolate mixture is very stiff; keep cutting and folding until it is incorporated. Pour into prepared tin and place in a roasting tin. Add boiling water to come halfway up tin, cover and bake in the oven for 1¹⁄₂ hours. Cool. When ready to serve, whip cream stiffly. Turn dessert out onto a serving dish and decorate with piped whipped cream.

Serves 6.

Turn out onto a serving plate. Whip cream stiffly in a bowl and pipe over top. Decorate with marrons glacés, if using. Let cake stand for 30 minutes at room temperature to soften before serving.

Serves 6-8.

Note: If butter is too hard to cream easily, add 1-2 teaspoons hot milk to it.

CHOCOLATE RING CAKE

90 g (3 oz) plain (dark) chocolate
60 g (2 oz/¼ cup) unsalted butter
2 tablespoons strong black coffee
185 g (6 oz/¾ cup) caster sugar
1 egg, separated, plus 1 extra white
½ teaspoon bicarbonate of soda
90 ml (3 fl oz/⅓ cup) whipping cream
155 g (5 oz/1¼ cups) plain flour
½ teaspoon baking powder

CHOCOLATE FROSTING: 125 g (4 oz) plain (dark)
  chocolate
155 ml (5 fl oz/⅔ cup) whipping cream
60 g (2 oz/¼ cup) butter
200 g (6½ oz/1 cup) icing sugar
few drops vanilla essence

In a large bowl, whisk egg whites until stiff, but not dry. Add 1 tablespoon to chocolate mixture, then pour chocolate mixture over egg whites and fold together. Pour into prepared tin and bake for 45-50 minutes, until set and spongy to touch. Leave the cake to cool in the tin.

Preheat oven to 180C (350F/Gas 4). Grease a 1.25 litre (40 fl oz/5 cup) savarin or ring mould and dust out with flour. Break chocolate and melt with butter and coffee in the top of a double boiler or a bowl set over a saucepan of simmering water. Add caster sugar and stir until dissolved.

To make the frosting, break the chocolate into pieces and put into a small saucepan. Add all remaining ingredients and stir over very gentle heat until chocolate and butter have melted and all the ingredients are thoroughly combined.

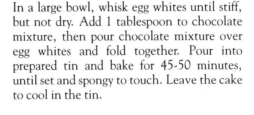

In a bowl, beat egg yolk with bicarbonate of soda and cream, and stir into chocolate. Sift flour and baking powder into chocolate mixture and fold together.

Turn cake out of the tin onto a serving plate. Quickly pour the frosting over cake and serve immediately while still warm.

Serves 10.

Note: For a special occasion, decorate with chocolate leaves and edible flowers. The frosting can be left to go cold, but it is nicest when served warm.

Variation: Omit frosting and serve cake with Dark Chocolate Sauce (see page 92).

— MIXED CHOCOLATE TERRINE —

WHITE CHOCOLATE MOUSSE: 280 g (9 oz) white
  chocolate
1½ teaspoons powdered gelatine
1 good tablespoon liquid glucose
2 egg yolks
155 ml (5 fl oz/⅔ cup) double (thick) cream
155 ml (5 fl oz/⅔ cup) thick sour cream

DARK CHOCOLATE MOUSSE: 185 g (6 oz) plain (dark)
  chocolate
4 tablespoons strong black coffee
2 teaspoons powdered gelatine
125 g (4 oz/½ cup) butter, cut into cubes
2 egg yolks
315 ml (10 fl oz/1¼ cups) whipping cream

To make dark chocolate mousse, melt chocolate with coffee in the top of a double boiler or a bowl set over a pan of simmering water. Sprinkle gelatine over 3 tablespoons water in a small bowl and leave to soften for 2-3 minutes. Stand bowl in a pan of hot water and stir until gelatine has dissolved. Stir into chocolate with butter and beat until butter has melted and everything is well mixed. Leave to cool, then beat in egg yolks. In a bowl, whip cream lightly and fold into chocolate mixture.

Line a 1 kg (2 lb) loaf tin with plastic wrap to overlap edges. To make the white chocolate mousse, break the white chocolate into small pieces and set aside. Sprinkle gelatine over 2 tablespoons water in a small bowl and leave to soften for 2-3 minutes. Put 3 tablespoons water in a saucepan with glucose and bring to the boil. Remove from heat and stir in gelatine until dissolved. Add chocolate and beat mixture until chocolate has melted and is smooth.

Pour dark chocolate mixture over set white chocolate mousse in terrine. Return to refrigerator until set, then cover with overlapping plastic wrap and place in the refrigerator overnight.

Beat in egg yolks, one at a time. In a bowl, whip the creams together lightly and fold into the chocolate mixture. Pour the chocolate into the loaf tin and refrigerate until set.

When ready to serve, unfold plastic wrap from top of mousse and turn out onto a serving dish. Carefully peel off plastic wrap and serve terrine cut in slices.

Serves 8-10.

Note: Decorate the terrine with whipped cream and grated chocolate, if desired. Either mousse can be served as a dessert on its own and will serve 4 people.

SAUCY CHOCOLATE PUDDINGS

90 g (3 oz) white chocolate
90 g (3 oz) milk chocolate
90 g (3 oz) plain (dark) chocolate
3 egg yolks
2 teaspoons finely grated grapefruit peel
2 teaspoons grapefruit juice
3 teaspoons Southern Comfort
3 teaspoons ginger wine
185 g (6 oz/¾ cup) softened butter
155 ml (5 fl oz/⅔ cup) double (thick) cream
9 teaspoons fromage frais

GRAPEFRUIT SAUCE: finely grated peel and juice of 1
grapefruit
2 teaspoons cornflour
3 teaspoons caster sugar

Break up chocolates and place in separate
bowls, each over a saucepan of hand-hot
water until melted. Stir an egg yolk into
each. Add grapefruit peel and juice to white
chocolate; Southern Comfort to plain (dark)
chocolate and ginger wine to milk chocolate;
stir until smooth. Leave to cool. Beat butter
until light and fluffy; whip cream and fromage
frais until thick. Fold ⅓ of each into the
chocolate mixtures. Line 6 dariole moulds
with plastic wrap. Divide milk chocolate
mixture between moulds.

Repeat with a white chocolate layer and
finally a dark chocolate layer. Tap moulds to
level and freeze until firm or until required.
To make sauce, make grapefruit juice and
peel up to 185 ml (6 fl oz/¾ cup) with water.
Blend with cornflour and sugar in a small
saucepan. Bring to boil, stirring; cook for 30
seconds; cool. Invert moulds onto serving
dishes 20 minutes before serving. Serve the
puddings with the cold sauce.

Makes 6.

STRAWBERRY BOXES

500 g (1 lb) plain dark chocolate
Whisked Sponge mixture made with 3 eggs, 90 g
(3 oz/⅓ cup) caster sugar and 90 g (3 oz/¾ cup)
self-raising flour (see page 68)
3-4 tablespoons strawberry jam, sieved
250 ml (8 fl oz/1 cup) whipping cream
caster sugar, to taste
250 g (8 oz) strawberries or fraise de bois, hulled

Melt the chocolate in the top of a double
boiler or a bowl set over a saucepan of
simmering water. Stir until smooth. Leave to
cool slightly, then spread onto greaseproof
paper to a 37.5 cm (15 in) square. Leave to
set at room temperature.

Bake cake in a 17.5 cm (7 in) square tin for
20-25 minutes. When cool, cut into sixteen
4 cm (1½ in) squares; trim as necessary.
Cut the chocolate into one hundred 4 cm
(1½ in) squares (this gives 6 for each cake
square and 4 spare in case any break). Warm
the jam slightly in a small saucepan, then
brush lightly all over sponge squares. Place
each one on a chocolate square. Press 4 more
chocolate squares round sides.

In a bowl, whip cream to stiff peaks and
sweeten with sugar. Slice strawberries if large;
leave fraise de bois whole. Carefully spoon
cream on top of sponge, then cover with
strawberries. Put a chocolate square on top of
each box to make a lid. Chill until required,
but serve within 1-2 hours.

Serves 8.

WHITE & PLAIN CHOC POTS

CHOCOLATE CUPS

125 g (4 oz) white chocolate
125 g (4 oz) plain (dark) chocolate
4 eggs, separated
3 teaspoons rum
3 teaspoons Cointreau
spirals of orange peel, to decorate, if desired

Break up each type of chocolate and place in separate bowls, each over a saucepan of hand-hot water. Stir occasionally until melted and smooth. Stir 2 egg yolks into each, then add rum to dark chocolate and Cointreau to white chocolate; stir until evenly blended.

In a bowl, stiffly whisk egg whites, then add ½ quantity to each of the chocolate mixtures. Fold in carefully until each mixture is evenly blended and smooth.

Place alternate spoonfuls of each mixture into 8 small glasses, or individual dishes. Leave in a cool place to set. Decorate with spirals of orange peel, if desired.

Makes 8.

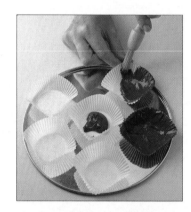

155 g (5 oz) white chocolate
juice and grated peel of 1 orange
1½ teaspoons powdered gelatine
2 eggs, separated
185 ml (6 fl oz/¾ cup) double (thick) cream
125 ml (4 fl oz/½ cup) thick sour cream

CUPS: 375 g (12 oz) plain (dark) chocolate
45 g (1½ oz/9 teaspoons) butter

To make cups, melt plain (dark) chocolate in the top of a double boiler or a bowl set over pan of simmering water. Stir in butter. Using a pastry bush, dab chocolate over base and sides of 12 cake cases.

Put cases into bun tins to support sides and refrigerate to harden. Meanwhile, melt white chocolate with half the orange juice in top of a double boiler or a bowl set over pan of simmering water. Sprinkle gelatine over remaining orange juice in a small bowl and leave to soften for 2-3 minutes. Stand bowl in saucepan of hot water and stir until gelatine has dissolved. Stir into chocolate with orange peel, then leave to cool.

Beat egg yolks into chocolate mixture. Whip creams together in a bowl. In a separate bowl, whisk egg whites until stiff. Fold cream, then egg whites into mixture and leave until on point of setting. Spoon into chocolate cups and refrigerate until mousse has set. Peel away cases before serving.

Serves 12.

Note: Decorate with blanched julienne strips of orange peel, if desired.

CAKE DESSERTS

VICTORIA SPONGE

125 g (4 oz/½ cup) soft tub margarine or butter,
  softened
125 g (4 oz/½ cup) caster sugar
2 large eggs
125 g (4 oz/1 cup) self-raising flour
milk, if needed

TO SERVE: whipped cream
fresh fruit

Preheat oven to 180C (350F/Gas 4). Grease
two 17.5 cm (7 in) round sandwich tins or a
20 cm (8 in) square tin.

In a bowl, cream margarine or butter and
sugar together until light and fluffy. Beat eggs
in a separate small bowl, then beat into
mixture a little at a time. Sift flour into
mixture and fold in using a metal spoon.
Mixture should be a soft dropping
consistency -- add a little milk if necessary.
Spoon into prepared tin(s). Bake in the oven
for about 15 or 25 minutes, depending on tin
size, until top is golden and spongy to touch.
Turn out and cool on a wire rack.

To serve, spread whipped cream on one round
cake and arrange fruit on top. Sandwich with
other cake. Spread a square cake with
whipped cream mixed with some fruit, and
arrange remainder over top.

Serves 6.

Variations: Beat a few drops of vanilla
essence or 1 tablespoon grated orange or
lemon peel into mixture before adding flour.
Ice the cake with water icing, or flavoured
butter icing, if desired.

CHERRY SPONGE FLANS

1 quantity of Victoria Sponge mixture (see left)
500 g (1 lb) fresh cherries, stoned
1 tablespoon caster sugar
1 teaspoon arrowroot
1 tablespoon kirsch
315 ml (10 fl oz/1¼ cups) whipping cream

Preheat oven to 180C (350F/Gas 4). Grease
8 individual 10 cm (4 in) Yorkshire pudding
tins. Divide the sponge mixture between
prepared tins and bake for 5-10 minutes, until
golden and spongy to touch.

Leave in tins to cool. Put cherries into a
saucepan with sugar. Cover pan and cook
over low heat until juices run. Mix arrowroot
to a smooth paste with 1 tablespoon water
and add to cherries. Bring to boil, stirring,
then remove from heat and leave to cool. Stir
in kirsch.

When ready to serve, place sponges on
individual serving plates. Spoon cherries in
their thick sauce on top. In a bowl, whip
cream stiffly and pipe a border round the
cherries. Serve immediately.

Serves 8.

Note: Arrowroot is a thickening agent like
cornflour, but it does not turn a sauce cloudy.
It is more usually used than cornflour to
thicken sweet sauces.

HOT ORANGE CAKE

125 g (4 oz/½ cup) butter, softened
125 g (4 oz/½ cup) caster sugar
2 large eggs, separated
125 g (4 oz/1 cup) self-raising flour
juice and grated peel of 3 small oranges
250 ml (8 fl oz/1 cup) double (thick) cream
icing sugar
fresh orange segments

Preheat oven to 180C (350F/Gas 4). Well grease a deep 20 cm (8 in) non-stick cake tin. In a large bowl, cream butter and sugar until light and fluffy. Beat egg yolks into mixture with 1 tablespoon flour and juice and grated peel of 1 orange.

In a separate bowl, whisk egg whites until stiff, but not dry. Fold into mixture with remaining flour and spoon into the prepared cake tin. Bake in the oven for 20-30 minutes, until golden brown and springy to touch.

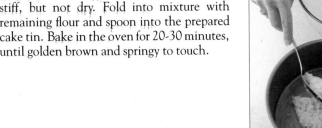

While cake is cooking, whip cream stiffly in a bowl with remaining orange juice and peel. Leave cake in tin for 2-3 minutes, then turn out and cut in half horizontally. Working quickly, spread bottom with cream, cover with top half. Dust thickly with icing sugar and arrange orange segments on top. Serve the cake at once.

Serves 6.

Note: The cream will melt into the hot cake, so serve as quickly as possible.

SPIKY COFFEE BRANDY CAKE

1 quantity of Victoria Sponge mixture (see opposite)
2 tablespoons brandy
3 teaspoons caster sugar
315 ml (10 fl oz/1¼ cups) hot strong black coffee
315 ml (10 fl oz/1¼ cups) whipping cream
3 teaspoons icing sugar
60 g (2 oz/½ cup) split almonds, toasted

Preheat oven to 180C (350F/Gas 4). Bake cake in a 625 ml (20 fl oz/2½ cup) greased pudding bowl and leave to cool in the bowl.

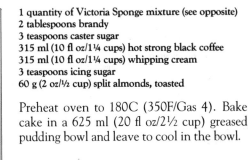

When cake is cold, stir brandy and caster sugar into hot coffee and pour over cake (still in the bowl). Put a saucer over the bowl and refrigerate overnight.

About 2 hours before serving, run a knife around edges of cake, then turn out onto a serving plate. In a bowl, whip cream with icing sugar until very stiff and spread evenly over cake, covering completely. Refrigerate. Immediately before serving, stick toasted almonds into surface of cream all over cake.

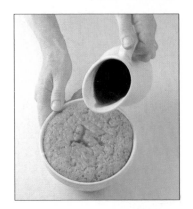

Serves 4-6.

Variation: For a special occasion, pipe rosettes of cream all over the cake, then decorate with almonds and flowers.

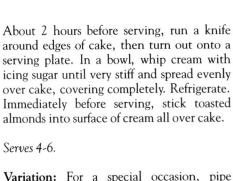

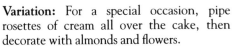

FRUIT CASKET

WHISKED SPONGE: 6 eggs
185 g (6 oz/¾ cup) caster sugar
finely grated peel of 1 lemon or small orange
185 g (6 oz/1½ cups) self-raising flour
icing sugar, to serve

FILLING: 315 ml (10 fl oz/1¼ cups) whipping cream
1 tablespoon kirsch
caster sugar, to taste
250 g (8 oz) raspberries
450 g (1 lb) strawberries

Preheat oven to 180C (350F/Gas 4). Grease a 22.5 cm (9 in) cake tin and dust with caster sugar and then flour.

In a large bowl, whisk the eggs, sugar and lemon or orange peel together until very thick, pale and mousse-like. Setting the bowl over a saucepan of gently simmering water helps with the whisking, but continue to whisk until the mixture is cold.

Sift flour twice onto a plate, then carefully, but thoroughly, fold into egg mixture. Pour into the prepared tin. Bake in the oven for 15-20 minutes, until lightly golden and springy to touch. Cool on a wire rack.

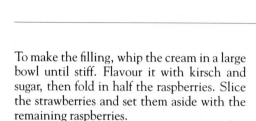

To make the filling, whip the cream in a large bowl until stiff. Flavour it with kirsch and sugar, then fold in half the raspberries. Slice the strawberries and set them aside with the remaining raspberries.

Cut sponge in half horizontally through middle. Put one half on serving dish. Cut a square out of centre of other half to leave a 2.5 cm (1 inch) unbroken frame.

Place this exactly on top of cake half. Fill frame with the cream mixture and top with strawberries and remaining raspberries. Cut remaining piece of sponge in half diagonally and set on top like butterfly wings. Dust with icing sugar and serve within 1 hour.

Serves 8.

Variation: Decorate the cake with cream, toasted flaked almonds and strawberry slices.

RUM TRUFFLE CAKE

220 g (7 oz) plain (dark) chocolate
125 g (4 oz/½ cup) unsalted butter
75 ml (2½ fl oz/⅓ cup) dark rum
3 eggs, separated
125 g (4 oz/½ cup) caster sugar
90 g (3 oz/¾ cup) plain flour
60 g (2 oz/½ cup) ground almonds

ICING: 220 g (7 oz) plain (dark) chocolate
315 ml (10 fl oz/1¼ cups) double (thick) cream
3 teaspoons dark rum
60 g (2 oz) white chocolate, grated

Butter and flour a 20 cm (8 in) round cake tin and line base with greaseproof paper.

Preheat oven to 180C (350F/Gas 4). Place chocolate and butter in a bowl over a saucepan of hand-hot water. Stir occasionally until melted. Add rum and stir well.

Place egg yolks and sugar in a bowl over a saucepan of simmering water. Whisk until thick and pale, remove bowl from pan and continue to whisk until mixture leaves a trail when whisk is lifted. Stir in chocolate mixture until evenly blended. Mix together flour and ground almonds, add to mixture and fold in carefully using a spatula.

Whisk egg whites until stiff, fold in ⅓ at a time until all egg white has been incorporated. Pour mixture into tin and bake in the oven for 45-55 minutes until firm to touch in centre. Turn out of tin and cool on a wire rack.

To make the icing, melt 125 g (4 oz) of the chocolate with 60 ml (2 fl oz/¼ cup) cream in a bowl over a pan of hot water. Stir in rum until well blended. Leave to cool. Whip 125 ml (4 fl oz/½ cup) cream in a bowl until thick, add ½ chocolate rum mixture and fold in to make a smooth icing.

Cut cake in half, sandwich together with the chocolate icing and spread remainder over top and sides. Chill cake and remaining ½ of chocolate rum mixture until firm. Melt remaining chocolate and cream in a bowl, stir until smooth; cool and pour mixture over cake to cover evenly. Shape firmed chocolate rum mixture into 16 truffles, coat in grated white chocolate. Arrange on top of cake; chill to set.

Makes 10-12 slices.

GRIESTORTE

3 eggs, separated
100 g (3½ oz/⅓ cup plus 3 teaspoons) caster sugar
grated peel of 1 orange
juice of ½ lemon
60 g (2 oz/⅓ cup) fine semolina
30 g (1 oz/¼ cup) ground almonds
250 ml (8 fl oz/1 cup) whipping cream
250 g (8 oz) raspberries
icing sugar, to serve

Preheat oven to 180C (350F/Gas 4). In a bowl, beat egg yolks, sugar and orange peel.

When mixture is light and fluffy, beat in lemon juice, semolina and almonds. In a separate bowl, whisk egg whites until stiff; fold into mixture. Pour into a deep 20 cm (8 in) non-stick cake tin and bake in the oven for 35 minutes, until golden brown and firm to the touch. Turn out of tin and cool on a wire rack. Whip cream in a bowl until stiff. Cut cold cake in half horizontally and spread bottom half with half the cream.

Arrange raspberries over cream, reserving a few for decoration. Top with other half of cake. Dust top with icing sugar and use remaining cream to pipe a border of rosettes. Decorate with reserved raspberries.

Serves 6.

Note: Another way to decorate with icing sugar, is to lay strips of greaseproof paper over the cake in a lattice pattern. Dust with icing sugar, then remove strips.

STRAWBERRY SHORTCAKE

125 g (4 oz/½ cup) butter, softened
60 g (2 oz/¼ cup) caster sugar
155 g (5 oz/1¼ cups) plain flour
30 g (1 oz/3 tablespoons) cornflour
375 g (12 oz) strawberries, hulled, and halved if large
3 tablespoons redcurrant jelly
315 ml (10 fl oz/1¼ cups) whipping cream

Preheat oven to 180C (350F/Gas 4). In a bowl, cream butter and sugar together until light and fluffy. Sift flour and cornflour together into creamy mixture and stir to make a firm dough.

Wrap in foil and chill for 30 minutes. Put dough onto a baking sheet and pat or roll it to a circle, about 1 cm (½ in) thick. Prick all over with a fork and bake in the oven for about 20 minutes, until lightly golden. Leave on baking sheet to cool.

Carefully transfer the shortcake to a serving plate and cover with the strawberries. Melt redcurrant jelly in a small saucepan and brush it over the strawberries. Whip cream stiffly in a bowl and use to pipe a border round edge of shortcake. Serve within 1 hour.

Serves 6-8.

ORANGE ROULADE

5 eggs, separated
185 g (6 oz/¾ cup) caster sugar, plus extra to sweeten
    cream
grated peel and juice of 2 oranges
icing sugar
315 ml (10 fl oz/1¼ cups) whipping cream
fresh orange segments, to decorate
Raspberry Sauce (see page 91), to serve, if desired

Preheat oven to 180C (350F/Gas 4). Line a swiss roll tin with double thickness foil and grease very well. In a bowl, whisk egg yolks, sugar and orange peel until thick.

In a large bowl, whisk egg whites until stiff but not dry. Fold 1 tablespoon into egg yolk mixture, then tip egg yolk mixture onto whites and fold together carefully. Pour into prepared tin and spread evenly. Bake in the oven for 30 minutes, remove from oven and immediately cover with a damp tea towel. When quite cold, turn onto a piece of foil thickly dusted with icing sugar. Peel off bottom layer of foil, in long, thin strips.

In a bowl, whip cream lightly and sweeten to taste. Gradually add orange juice, whisking all the time, until stiff. Reserve a little cream for decoration and spread remainder evenly over sponge. Roll up, using the foil to help and transfer to a serving plate. Pipe rosettes along sides using reserved cream and decorate with fresh orange segments. Serve with Raspberry Sauce, if using.

Serves 6.

RASPBERRY ROULADE

185 g (6 oz/1⅔ cups) hazelnuts
5 eggs, separated
155 g (5 oz/⅔ cup) caster sugar
icing sugar
315 ml (10 fl oz/1¼ cups) whipping cream
375 g (12 oz) raspberries
125 ml (4 fl oz/½ cup) double (thick) cream

Heat oven to 180C (350F/Gas 4). Line a swiss roll tin with double thickness foil and oil thoroughly. Grind hazelnuts finely in a coffee grinder or food processor.

In a large bowl, whisk egg yolks with sugar until thick and mousse-like. Fold in ground hazelnuts. In a separate bowl, whisk egg whites until stiff but not dry. Fold carefully into nut mixture, then pour into prepared tin and spread evenly. Bake in the oven for 15-20 minutes, until risen and firm to touch. Cover immediately with a damp tea towel and leave overnight. The next day, turn out onto a sheet of foil thickly dusted with icing sugar. Peel off foil.

In a bowl, whip whipping cream to stiff peaks. In a separate bowl, lightly crush half the raspberries, then fold into cream. Spread mixture over roulade. Reserve 6 raspberries, and dot remainder over the cream, then roll up the roulade using the foil to help. Transfer to a serving plate. Whip double (thick) cream thickly and use to pipe 6 large rosettes along the top of the roulade. Top each cream rosette with a raspberry.

Serves 6.

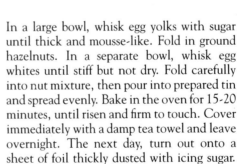

CHOCOLATE CHERRY SLICE

185 g (6 oz) plain (dark) chocolate
4 eggs
60 g (2 oz/¼ cup) caster sugar
45 g (1½ oz/¼ cup) plain flour
FILLING: 220 g (7 oz/1 cup) unsweetened chestnut purée
125 g (4 oz) plain (dark) chocolate, melted
315 ml (10 fl oz/1¼ cups) double (thick) cream
9 teaspoons Morello cherry jam
185 g (6 oz/1 cup) fresh or canned cherries, stoned and halved

Preheat oven to 190C (375F/Gas 5). Line a 32.5 x 22.5 cm (13 x 9 in) Swiss roll tin with non-stick paper.

Melt chocolate in a bowl over a pan of hand-hot water. Whisk eggs and sugar until pale and thick enough to leave a trail. Stir in chocolate; sift in flour and fold in gently. Transfer to tin, shake to level and bake in the oven for 20-25 minutes until firm to touch. Cover with a damp tea towel; leave until cold. To make filling, put chestnut purée and chocolate in a food processor fitted with a metal blade. Process until puréed. Fold in ⅔ cream. Stiffly whip remaining cream; place in a piping bag fitted with a small star nozzle.

Turn cake out of tin; remove paper. Trim edges and cut into 3 short strips across width. Spread 2 strips of cake with jam, then cover with ⅓ chestnut mixture. Arrange ⅓ cherry halves on each; stack layers together on a serving plate with remaining cake layer on top. Spread top and sides with remaining chestnut mixture and pipe cream around top edge. Decorate with remaining cherry halves. Chill.

Serves 10.

PLUM & APPLE KUCHEN

315 g (10 oz) packet white bread mix
185 ml (6 fl oz/¾ cup) warm water
30 g (1 oz/6 teaspoons) butter, melted
90 g (3 oz/¾ cup) ground almonds
60 g (2 oz/¼ cup) caster sugar
1 teaspoon ground mixed spice
500 g (1 lb) cooking apples, peeled, cored and sliced
1 kg (2 lb) plums, stoned and halved
90 ml (3 fl oz/⅓ cup) plum jam, boiled and sieved
3 teaspoons flaked almonds

Preheat oven to 220C (425F/Gas 7). Place bread mix in a bowl.

Add warm water according to instructions on packet. Knead dough until smooth; cover and leave for 5 minutes. Re-knead dough and roll out to a 30 cm (12 in) round on a lightly floured surface. Place in a buttered 25 cm (10 in) flan tin, or on a baking sheet, and brush dough with butter. In a bowl, mix together ground almonds, sugar and mixed spice. Sprinkle over dough.

Arrange apple slices and plum halves neatly over almond mixture. Bake in the oven for 20-30 minutes until dough is well risen and filling is tender. Cool on a wire rack, then brush with plum jam to glaze, and sprinkle with flaked almonds.

Serves 12.

PASTRY DESSERTS

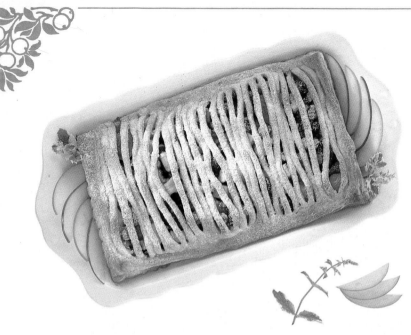

MINCEMEAT JALOUSIE

410 g (13 oz) puff pastry, thawed if frozen
1 tablespoon milk
1 tablespoon caster sugar

MINCEMEAT: 2 eating apples
2 bananas
juice and grated peel of ½ lemon and 1 orange
60 g (2 oz) grapes
90 g (3 oz/⅔ cup) currants
90 g (3 oz/½ cup) raisins
90 g (3 oz/½ cup) sultanas
30 g (1 oz/¼ cup) almonds, roughly chopped
30 g (1 oz/⅓ cup) walnuts, roughly chopped
30 g (1 oz/⅓ cup) raw cane sugar
2 tablespoons brandy
45 g (1½ oz/9 teaspoons) butter, melted

To make the mincemeat, peel and chop apples and bananas. In a large bowl, quickly toss prepared fruit in lemon juice. Halve and seed grapes and add to fruit with orange juice and lemon and orange peel. Add currants, raisins and sultanas. Add nuts to mixture with sugar and brandy. Mix everything together well, then stir in melted butter. You only need one-third of this quantity for the jalousie, but it is not worth making a smaller amount. Use the remainder for mince pies.

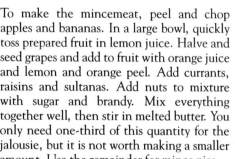

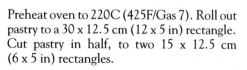

Preheat oven to 220C (425F/Gas 7). Roll out pastry to a 30 x 12.5 cm (12 x 5 in) rectangle. Cut pastry in half, to two 15 x 12.5 cm (6 x 5 in) rectangles.

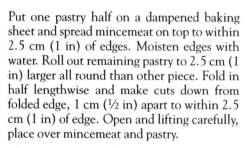

Put one pastry half on a dampened baking sheet and spread mincemeat on top to within 2.5 cm (1 in) of edges. Moisten edges with water. Roll out remaining pastry to 2.5 cm (1 in) larger all round than other piece. Fold in half lengthwise and make cuts down from folded edge, 1 cm (½ in) apart to within 2.5 cm (1 in) of edge. Open and lifting carefully, place over mincemeat and pastry.

Press edges of pastry together and 'knock up' sides using a blunt knife. Chill jalousie for 30 minutes. Brush lightly with milk and sprinkle with caster sugar. Bake in the oven for 30-35 minutes, until pastry is puffed up and golden.

If the pastry starts to brown too quickly, cover it with foil.

Serves 6.

Note: Serve the jalousie with 250 ml (8 fl oz/ 1 cup) whipping cream, whipped with 1 tablespoon brandy and 1 tablespoon caster sugar.

The mincemeat can be made in advance and stored in a rigid plastic container in the refrigerator for up to 5 days.

INDIVIDUAL PEAR PUFFS

STRAWBERRY MILLE FEUILLE

250 g (8 oz) puff pastry, thawed if frozen
2 large, ripe eating pears
1 egg yolk
1 tablespoon milk
caster sugar for sprinkling
Poire William liqueur, if desired

Preheat oven to 220C (425F/Gas 7). Roll out pastry to a rough rectangle, about 0.5 cm (¼ in) thick. Using a pear (halved, if easier) as a guide, cut out a pastry pear shape, 1 cm (½ in) larger than the pear.

410 g (13 oz) puff pastry, thawed if frozen
500 g (1 lb) fresh strawberries
315 ml (10 fl oz/1¼ cups) whipping cream
1-2 drops vanilla essence
caster sugar, to taste
5 tablespoons redcurrant jelly

Preheat oven to 220C (425F/Gas 7). Roll out the pastry to a thin rectangle and cut it into 3 even sections.

Cut directly round pear, leaving a pear-shaped 'frame'. Roll out solid pear shape to same size as frame, dampen edges with water and fit frame on top. Press edges together lightly, then 'knock up' using a blunt knife. Make 3 more pastry pear shapes in same way. Peel and halve pears. Scoop out cores with a teaspoon, then cut across into thin slices. Fit neatly into pastry shapes.

Place sections on baking sheets and prick all over with a fork. Bake in the oven for 15-20 minutes, until golden brown and crisp. Cool on a wire rack. When cold, trim edges with a very sharp knife to make even. Reserve trimmings. Cut half of the strawberries in half – choose even-sized ones for this. Slice remainder. In a bowl, whip cream fairly stiffly and flavour with vanilla essence and sugar. Fold sliced strawberries into cream.

Place pear puffs on baking sheet. Beat egg yolk with milk in a small bowl and brush edges of pastry with this. Bake in the oven for 15-20 minutes, until pears are tender and pastry edges are puffed up and golden. Remove from oven, sprinkle with caster sugar and place under a hot grill for 1 minute. Transfer to serving plates. Heat liqueur, if using, in a small saucepan, set alight and pour, flaming, over puffs. Serve at once.

Serves 4.

Put a pastry slice onto a serving plate and spread with half the cream mixture. Lay another slice on top and spread with remaining cream mixture. Top with third slice. Put redcurrant jelly and 2 tablespoons water into a small saucepan and heat gently until jelly has dissolved. Brush top slice with a little jelly and arrange halved strawberries on top. Brush with remainder of jelly. Crush reserved pastry trimmings and press into sides of slice with the blade of a knife.

Serves 6-8.

TARTE FRANÇAISE

KUMQUAT CRANBERRY TARTS

410 g (13 oz) puff pastry, thawed if frozen
1 egg yolk, beaten
6 tablespoons apricot jam, sieved
2 tablespoons lemon juice
about 750 g (1½ lb) mixed fresh fruit, such as grapes,
   strawberries and/or raspberries and bananas

Preheat oven to 220C (425F/Gas 7). Roll out pastry to a 30 x 20 cm (12 x 8 in) rectangle. Fold pastry in half, to a 15 x 20 cm (6 x 8 in) rectangle. Cut a rectangle from folded edge, 4 cm (1½ in) in from outside edges.

WALNUT PASTRY: 185 g (6 oz/1½ cups) plain flour
125 g (4 oz/½ cup) butter
60 g (2 oz/½ cup) chopped walnuts
60 g (2 oz/¼ cup) caster sugar
1 egg, beaten

FILLING: 185 g (6 oz/¾ cup) caster sugar
250 g (8 oz) kumquats, sliced
250 g (8 oz/1½ cups) cranberries
185 g (6 oz/¾ cup) cream cheese
90 ml (3 fl oz/⅓ cup) Greek yogurt
1 teaspoon arrowroot

To make pastry, sift the flour into a bowl.

Unfold middle section and roll out to same size as 'frame' – 30 x 20 cm (12 x 8 in). Place on a baking sheet, dampen edges with water, then unfold 'frame' and place carefully on top of pastry rectangle. Press edges of pastry together, then 'knock up' using a blunt knife. Mark a pattern on frame and brush with beaten egg yolk. Prick centre of case all over.

Add butter and rub in to form breadcrumbs. Stir in walnuts, sugar and enough egg to form a soft dough. Knead and roll out to line six 12 cm (4½ in) fluted flan tins. Trim edges and prick bases; chill 30 minutes. Preheat oven to 190C (375F/Gas 5). Heat sugar and 250 ml (8 fl oz/1 cup) water until dissolved. Bring to boil, add kumquats; cook for 3 minutes. Strain; return ⅓ syrup to pan; reserve remaining syrup. Add cranberries to syrup in pan, bring to boil, cover and cook for 3 minutes.

Leave pastry in a cool place for 10 minutes, then bake for about 20 minutes, until golden brown. Leave to cool. Put jam and lemon juice into a saucepan and heat gently until jam has melted. To prepare fruit, halve and seed grapes, leave strawberries and/or raspberries whole and peel and slice bananas. Brush base of tart lightly with jam and arrange fruit in rows. Brush fruit with jam and serve as soon as possible.

Serves 6.

Strain, keeping individual syrups and fruit separate. Bake tart cases in oven for 10-15 minutes until lightly browned. Cool. Beat cream cheese with yogurt. Spread over base of tarts. Arrange alternate circles of fruit in tarts. Blend ½ teaspoon arrowroot into each syrup; bring each to boil. Glaze kumquats with clear syrup and cranberries with red syrup. Leave to set.

Serves 6.

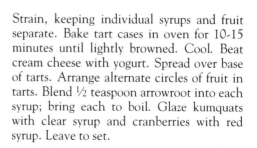

TREACLE CREAM FLAN

SHORTCRUST PASTRY: 250 g (8 oz/2 cups) plain flour
pinch of salt
125 g (4 oz/½ cup) butter, cut into cubes
1 teaspoon sugar, if desired
2-3 tablespoons chilled water or milk

FILLING: 8 tablespoons golden syrup
45 g (1½ oz/9 teaspoons) butter, cut into cubes
4 tablespoons thick sour cream
grated peel of 1 lemon
2 eggs, beaten

Sift flour and salt into a bowl. Using fingertips, rub butter into flour until mixture resembles breadcrumbs.

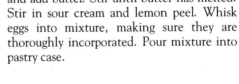

Stir in sugar, to make a sweet pastry if desired. Then, using a round-bladed knife, stir in sufficient water or milk to make a firm, but not sticky dough. Knead lightly on a floured surface. Wrap pastry in plastic wrap or foil and put in a cool place for 30 minutes. Resting pastry allows the flour to expand and helps to prevent pastry shrinking during cooking. Preheat oven to 190C (375F/Gas 5).

Unwrap the pastry and roll out on a lightly floured surface so that it is a good 2.5 cm (1 in) bigger all round than a 20 cm (8 in) flan ring or flan tin. Lift pastry on a rolling pin and lower into flan tin. Press gently into sides and trim off any excess with a sharp knife.

To bake blind, fold foil into 2.5 cm (1 in) strips using several thicknesses of foil and press round sides of pastry case. Prick base, then bake in the oven for 15-20 minutes, until dry and lightly coloured. Cool. Lower oven temperature to 180C (350F/Gas 4).

To make filling, warm syrup in a medium saucepan over a low heat. Remove from heat and add butter. Stir until butter has melted. Stir in sour cream and lemon peel. Whisk eggs into mixture, making sure they are thoroughly incorporated. Pour mixture into pastry case.

Bake the flan in the oven for 45-55 minutes, until filling is golden brown and puffed up. Serve warm or cold.

Serves 6.

Note: Serve the flan with whipped double (thick) cream and decorate with lemon slices or strips of peel and fresh herbs, if desired.

PECAN PIE

1 quantity of Shortcrust Pastry (see page 77)
3 eggs
315 g (10 oz/2 cups) soft brown sugar
1 tablespoon clear honey
30 g (1 oz/6 teaspoons) butter, melted
2 tablespoons whipping cream
pinch of salt
185 g (6 oz/1½ cups) pecan nuts, roughly chopped
icing sugar to serve, if desired

Preheat the oven to 190C (375F/Gas 5). Use the pastry to line a 25 cm (10 in) flan tin and bake blind as directed on page 77. Leave oven at 190C (375F/Gas 5).

In a large bowl, whisk eggs and brown sugar together until pale and thick. Stir in honey, butter, whipping cream and salt and mix together thoroughly. Fold in pecan nuts.

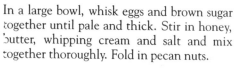

Pour mixture evenly into baked pastry case and bake in the oven for 20 minutes. Lower oven temperature to 160C (325F/Gas 3) and cook for a further 45-50 minutes, until set. Serve warm, or allow to cool, and serve chilled. Dust with icing sugar, if desired.

Serves 6.

Note: Substitute walnuts for pecans in this pie if you prefer, or if you have difficulty in obtaining pecan nuts.

ORANGE MERINGUE PIE

1 quantity of Shortcrust Pastry (see page 77)
45 g (1½ oz/12 teaspoons) cornflour
315 ml (10 fl oz/1¼ cups) water
30 g (1 oz/6 teaspoons) butter
juice and grated peel of 2 small oranges
juice and grated peel of 1 small lime
2 eggs, separated
185 g (6 oz/¾ cup) caster sugar

Preheat oven to 190C (375F/Gas 5). Use the pastry to line a 25 cm (10 in) flan tin and bake blind as described on page 77. Lower oven to 160C (325F/Gas 3).

In a bowl, mix cornflour to a smooth paste with a little of the water. Stir in remaining water, then pour into a saucepan and add butter. Bring to the boil, stirring constantly. Simmer for 2-3 minutes, still stirring, then remove from heat. Beat in fruit juices and grated peel, egg yolks and one-third of the sugar. Spoon into flan case and cool slightly.

In a large bowl, whisk egg whites until stiff but not dry, add half remaining sugar and whisk again until mixture holds its shape. Fold in rest of sugar, then spoon or pipe meringue on top of flan, to cover filling and pastry. Bake in the oven for 20-30 minutes, until meringue is set and lightly golden. Serve warm or cold.

Serves 6-8.

CLEMENTINE TARTLETS

CHOCOLATE PROFITEROLES

1 quantity of Shortcrust Pastry (see page 77)
juice of 2 oranges and 1 lemon
470 g (15 oz/2¼ cups) caster sugar
4 clementines
2 eggs, plus 2 extra yolks
125 g (4 oz/½ cup) butter, softened
1 heaped tablespoon ground almonds
2-3 tablespoons Grand Marnier or Cointreau

CHOUX PASTRY: 60 g (2 oz/¼ cup) butter, cubed
75 g (2½ oz/⅝ cup) plain flour, sifted
2 eggs, beaten

TO SERVE: 315 ml (10 fl oz/1¼ cups) whipping cream
Hot Dark Chocolate Sauce (see page 92)

Preheat the oven to 190C (375F/Gas 5). Use the pastry to line six 12.5 cm (5 in) tartlet tins and bake blind for 10-15 minutes as described on page 77. Leave oven temperature at 190 (375F/Gas 5).

Preheat oven to 200C (400F/Gas 6). Line 2 baking sheets with silicone paper. Put butter and 155 ml (5 fl oz/⅔ cup) water into a saucepan and set over a medium heat. When butter has melted, bring to boil; remove from heat. Add flour and beat until mixture leaves sides of pan.

Put orange and lemon juice into a saucepan with 280 g (9 oz/1¼ cups) sugar. Set over a medium heat until sugar has dissolved, then boil syrup for 15 minutes. Peel clementines, cut into slices and add to syrup. Simmer gently for 2-3 minutes. Remove clementines to a plate with a slotted spoon and boil syrup until very thick and syrupy. Set aside. In a bowl, beat eggs, extra yolks and remaining sugar together until well mixed. Beat in butter, almonds and liqueur.

Beat in eggs gradually until mixture is smooth and shiny (do this in a food processor for speed and ease). Put mixture into a piping bag and pipe walnut-sized blobs onto prepared baking sheets. Bake in the oven for 20-25 minutes, until brown, puffed up and just crisp on the outside. Make a small hole in side of each profiterole; this allows steam to escape and helps keep them crisp.

Divide mixture between tartlets and bake for about 8 minutes, until set and golden. Set aside to cool. When cold, brush tartlets with a little thick syrup and arrange clementine slices on top (halve the slices for a dainter effect, if preferred). Brush with a little more syrup, then chill until required.

Serves 6.

Variation: Use strawberries or blackberries instead of clementines, but immerse in syrup for a few seconds only.

Cool profiteroles on a wire rack. When ready to serve, whip cream stiffly. Enlarge hole in side of each profiterole and pipe cream into them. Serve profiteroles with the hot sauce poured over them.

Serves 4.

SALAMBOS

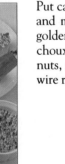

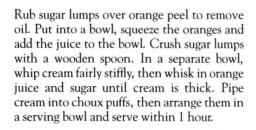

1 quantity of Choux Pastry (see page 79)
60 g (2 oz/½ cup) chopped mixed nuts
185 g (6 oz/¾ cup) caster sugar
5-6 sugar lumps
1 orange
315 ml (10 fl oz/1¼ cups) whipping cream

Preheat the oven to 200C (400F/Gas 6). Cook choux pastry as for Chocolate Profiteroles (see page 79). Brown the nuts in an ovenproof dish at the same time, turning occasionally to brown evenly. Leave to cool.

Put caster sugar into a heavy-based saucepan and melt over a very low heat. Cook to a golden brown caramel. Quickly dip each choux puff into the caramel and then into the nuts, coating them quite thickly. Replace on wire rack and leave caramel to harden.

Rub sugar lumps over orange peel to remove oil. Put into a bowl, squeeze the oranges and add the juice to the bowl. Crush sugar lumps with a wooden spoon. In a separate bowl, whip cream fairly stiffly, then whisk in orange juice and sugar until cream is thick. Pipe cream into choux puffs, then arrange them in a serving bowl and serve within 1 hour.

Serves 4.

BEIGNETS

1 quantity of Choux Pastry (see page 79)
oil for deep frying
caster sugar
Raspberry Sauce (see page 91), Mincemeat Sauce (see page 92) or Hot Lemon Sauce (see page 93)

Make up choux pastry as described on page 79 but set aside after adding eggs. Heat oil for deep frying to 180C (350F).

Drop teaspoonfuls of pastry into the hot fat. As beignets swell, turn up heat under pan so temperature rises to 190C (375F), see **Note**. Cook until puffed up and golden all over. Drain well on crumpled absorbent kitchen paper and keep them warm while cooking the remainder.

Toss warm beignets in caster sugar to coat lightly and serve with chosen sauce.

Serves 4.

Note: Oil should not be at its hottest when beignets first go into it, or they will swell too quickly and the inside will not be cooked.

AUTUMN FRUIT GOUGÈRE

1 quantity of Choux Pastry (see page 79)
500 g (1 lb) cooking apples
30 g (1 oz/6 teaspoons) butter
250 g (8 oz) fresh or frozen blackberries, thawed if frozen
30 g (1 oz/6 teaspoons) demerara sugar
315 ml (10 fl oz/1¼ cups) whipping cream
icing sugar, to serve

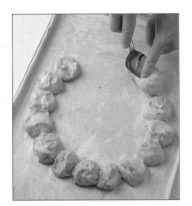

Bake pastry in the oven for 25-35 minutes, until puffed up and golden. Split circle in half horizontally and scoop out and discard any uncooked paste. Return halves, cut side up, to baking sheet and bake for a further 5 minutes. Leave to cool. Peel, core and slice apples. Melt butter in a saucepan and add apples, blackberries and demerara sugar. Cover and simmer gently until fruit is soft but not pulpy. Remove from heat and cool.

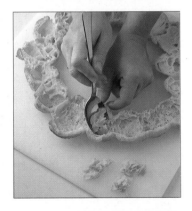

Place bottom half of pastry on a serving dish. Whip cream stiffly and spread in pastry. Spoon fruit mixture over cream and top with remaining pastry. Dust with icing sugar and serve immediately.

Serves 6.

Note: Pastry blobs should just touch each other – they will then join up during cooking. Do not smooth out blobs – the finished effect should be slightly rough.

APRICOT HAZELNUT GALETTE

90 g (3 oz/½ cup) hazelnuts, skinned
90 g (3 oz/⅓ cup) butter, softened
90 g (3 oz/⅓ cup) caster sugar
125 g (4 oz/1 cup) plain flour
250 g (8 oz) fresh apricots, halved and stoned
315 ml (10 fl oz/1¼ cups) whipping cream
icing sugar for dusting

Preheat oven to 180C (350F/Gas 4). Lightly grease 2 baking sheets. Toast hazelnuts under a medium grill to brown evenly. Reserve 8 nuts, then grind remainder finely in a coffee grinder or food processor.

In a bowl, beat butter and two-thirds sugar together until light and fluffy. Fold in ground nuts and flour, then beat to a firm dough. Knead lightly on a lightly floured surface, then wrap in foil and chill for 30 minutes. Unwrap, cut in half and roll each piece out to a 17.5-20 cm (7-8 in) diameter circle. Carefully place on the greased baking sheets and bake in the oven for about 20 minutes, until golden. Cut one circle into 8 wedges and cool all pastry on a wire rack.

Poach apricots gently in 3 tablespoons water and remaining sugar, until just soft. Cool. In a bowl, whip cream stiffly. Transfer pastry circle to a serving plate and spread with half the cream. Remove apricots from pan with a slotted spoon and arrange over cream. Top with pastry sections and dust with icing sugar. Pipe a rosette onto each section with remaining cream and decorate with hazelnuts. Serve within 1 hour.

Serves 8.

CREAM CHEESE STRUDEL

75 g (2½ oz/¾ cup) hazelnuts
250 g (8 oz) cream or curd cheese
2 tablespoons caster sugar
1 egg
grated peel of 1 lemon
5 sheets filo pastry, thawed if frozen
60 g (2 oz/¼ cup) butter, melted
icing sugar for dusting
Blackcurrant Sauce (see page 90), to serve

Preheat oven to 200C (400F/Gas 6). Grease a baking sheet. Toast hazelnuts under medium grill to brown evenly. Set aside to cool, then chop.

In a bowl, beat cheese with sugar, egg and lemon peel until smooth. Beat in hazelnuts. Place a sheet of pastry on greased baking sheet, keeping remainder covered with a damp tea towel. Brush with melted butter and place another sheet on top. Layer all 5 sheets of pastry on top of one another, brushing each one with melted butter.

Spoon cheese mixture in a line down centre of pastry and fold either short end over the filling. Roll up pastry, round filling, and turn it on baking sheet, so join is underneath. Brush top of strudel with remaining butter and bake in the oven for 25-30 minutes, until golden brown and flaky. Dust with icing sugar and serve warm, cut in diagonal slices. Serve the Blackcurrant Sauce separately.

Serves 4-6.

NECTARINE BAKLAVA

10 sheets filo pastry, thawed if frozen
155 g (5 oz/⅔ cup) butter, melted
220 g (7 oz/1¾ cups) chopped mixed nuts
1½ teaspoons ground cinnamon
8 tablespoons caster sugar
juice and grated peel of 2 lemons
1 tablespoon orange flower water
4 nectarines
icing sugar, to decorate

Preheat oven to 180C (350F/Gas 4). Cut pastry sheets in half, and each half into 4.

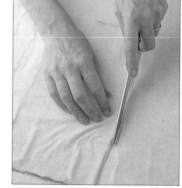

Working quickly, brush one cut sheet of pastry with melted butter. Line 8 individual 10 cm (4 in) Yorkshire pudding tins with one piece of pastry each. Brush 3 more cut sheets with butter and lay the pieces in the tins, so each tin has 4 pieces overlapping each other at different angles. Mix nuts, cinnamon and half the sugar, and spread half this mixture over pastry. Cover with 2 more layers of pastry, brushed with butter, then top with remaining nut mixture. Cover with rest of pastry, brushed with butter.

Press down pastry in tins and bake in the oven for 20-25 minutes, until golden brown. Meanwhile, dissolve remaining sugar in lemon juice over low heat. Stir in lemon peel and orange flower water. Bring to boil and simmer for 3 minutes. Cool slightly. Slice nectarines into syrup, turning them carefully to coat. Spoon into centre of pastries and dust edges with icing sugar. Serve lukewarm or cold, when pastries have absorbed some of the syrup.

Serves 8.

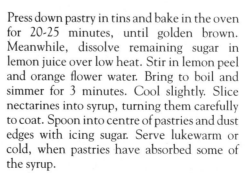

ICED DESSERTS

NUTTY BROWN BREAD CREAM

60 g (2 oz/½ cup) hazelnuts
75 g (2½ oz/1¼ cups) fresh brown breadcrumbs
30 g (1 oz/2 tablespoons) demerara sugar
2 egg whites
90 g (3 oz/⅓ cup) caster sugar
315 ml (10 fl oz/1¼ cups) whipping cream
1-2 drops vanilla essence

Toast hazelnuts evenly, cool, then grind coarsely in a coffee grinder. Mix with breadcrumbs and demerara sugar in a bowl.

Tip crumb mixture onto a baking sheet and spread out evenly. Grill under medium-hot grill, turning and shaking, until brown. Leave to cool. Whisk egg whites in a large bowl, until stiff. Sprinkle in sugar and whisk for a further 2 minutes. In a separate bowl, whip cream with vanilla essence to soft peaks, then fold into egg whites with all but 1 tablespoon of breadcrumb mixture.

Spoon mixture into 6 glasses and chill until ready to serve. Sprinkle with reserved crumb mixture just before serving.

Serves 6.

Note: This mixture makes a delicious ice cream; simply turn the finished cream into a plastic container and freeze.

LYCHEE SORBET

two 440 g (14 oz) cans lychees in syrup
juice and grated peel of 1 lemon
2 egg whites
mint sprigs, to decorate

Drain lychees, reserving 315 ml (10 fl oz/1¼ cups) syrup. Purée lychees with the syrup and lemon juice in a blender or food processor.

Stir in lemon peel, tip into a plastic container and freeze for about 1 hour, until mixture is slushy and semi-frozen.

In a large bowl, whisk egg whites until stiff. Tip in semi-frozen lychee purée and fold together to combine thoroughly. Return to freezer until firm. Serve the sorbet decorated with sprigs of mint.

Serves 4-6.

Note: If time permits, whisk sorbet once more about 1 hour after adding egg whites. This gives a smoother texture. Serve sorbets soon after making for the best flavour.

MANDARIN FIG SORBET

125 g (4 oz/½ cup) caster sugar
pared peel and juice of 4 mandarins
6 green figs
2 teaspoons powdered gelatine
2 egg whites
fig slices and mint sprigs, to decorate

Heat sugar and 155 ml (5 fl oz/⅔ cup) water in a saucepan, stirring occasionally until dissolved. Add mandarin peel and figs, bring to boil, then cover and simmer for 10 minutes. Leave until cold.

Remove mandarin peel and pour liquid and figs into a food processor and process until puréed. Sieve mixture. Sprinkle gelatine over 9 teaspoons water in a small bowl and leave to soften for 2-3 minutes. Stand bowl in a saucepan of hot water and stir until dissolved and quite hot. Add to fig purée with mandarin juice; stir well. Pour into a plastic container, cover and freeze for 2 hours or until partially frozen but still mushy.

Spoon mixture into a food processor and process until creamy, well blended and smooth. Stiffly whisk egg whites and fold into mixture. Return mixture to container, cover and freeze until firm, or until required. Place container of sorbet in refrigerator for 15 minutes to soften slightly before serving in scoops. Decorate with fig slices and mint.

Serves 6.

AMARETTI MERINGUE BOMBES

30 g (1 oz/6 teaspoons) butter, melted
20 Amaretti biscuits, crushed finely
375 g (12 oz) raspberries, thawed if frozen
4 teaspoons icing sugar
raspberries and Amaretti biscuits, to decorate

FILLING: 125 g (4 oz/2 cups) roughly crushed
    meringues
30 g (1 oz/¼ cup) Amaretti biscuits, broken into small
    pieces
60 g (2 oz/¼ cup) maraschino cherries, chopped
30 g (1 oz/¼ cup) chocolate dots (chips)
625 ml (20 fl oz/2½ cups) double (thick) cream

Brush 8 tiny moulds with melted butter.

Divide crushed Amaretti biscuits between moulds and shake well to coat evenly. Chill. To make filling, mix together meringues, Amaretti biscuits, cherries and chocolate in a bowl. Stir well. Whip cream until softly peaking, add meringue mixture and fold in very gently until evenly mixed. Fill each mould with meringue mixture, pressing well down to pack evenly. Cover and freeze until required.

Put raspberries and icing sugar in a food processor fitted with a metal blade and process until puréed. Sieve raspberry mixture into a jug. Just before serving, dip moulds into hand-hot water and invert onto serving plates. Decorate with a few raspberries and Amaretti biscuits and serve with raspberry sauce.

Makes 8.

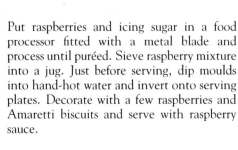

COFFEE BOMBE

ICED KIWI FRUIT TERRINE

3 eggs, separated
185 g (6 oz/¾ cup) caster sugar
75 ml (2½ fl oz/⅓ cup) cold strong black coffee
500 ml (16 fl oz/2 cups) double (thick) cream
155 g (5 oz) meringues
whipped cream and chocolate coffee beans, to decorate
hot Bitter Mocha Sauce (see page 90)

In a large bowl, beat egg yolks and sugar together until thick and mousse-like. Gently stir in coffee. In a separate bowl, whip cream lightly. Crush meringues.

1 quantity Passion Fruit Mousse (see page 29)
6 kiwi fruit
185 ml (6 fl oz/¾ cup) whipping cream

Lightly oil a 1 kg (2 lb) loaf tin. Make up mousse as directed on page 43 and spoon one-third of it into the bottom of the tin. Place in the freezer until set.

Fold cream and meringues into coffee mixture. In a large bowl, whisk egg whites until stiff and fold 1 tablespoon into coffee mixture. Tip egg whites onto coffee mixture, then fold together carefully. Pour into a 2 litre (64 fl oz/8 cup) lightly oiled bombe mould and freeze until firm.

Peel kiwi fruit and cut across fruit into thin slices. Arrange 2 of the sliced fruit over top of mousse in rows, then carefully spoon half remaining mousse on top. Freeze again, until set. Repeat process with 2 more sliced kiwi and top with remaining mousse. Return to the freezer until set.

One hour before serving, transfer the bombe to the refrigerator to soften slightly. Turn out onto a serving dish and decorate with cream and chocolate coffee beans. Serve with hot Bitter Mocha Sauce handed separately.

Serves 8.

Note: To turn out bombe, wring out a tea-towel in very hot water and wrap it around the mould. Invert onto a serving plate and lift off mould.

About 2 hours before serving, remove terrine from freezer and turn out onto a serving dish. In a bowl, whip cream stiffly, and use to pipe a 'ruff' down each side of terrine. Decorate with remaining 2 kiwi fruit.

Serves 6.

Note: Select kiwi fruit that give slightly when you squeeze them, but are not too soft.

ICED LOGANBERRY SOUFFLÉ

PINEAPPLE ALASKA

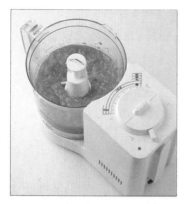

500 g (1 lb) loganberries or raspberries
lemon juice, to taste
155 g (5 oz/²⁄₃ cup) caster sugar
3 egg whites
470 ml (15 fl oz/1¾ cups) whipping cream
raspberries and mint sprigs, to decorate

Purée fruit in a blender or food processor, then sieve to remove seeds. Flavour with lemon juice.

Put sugar and 125 ml (4 fl oz/½ cup) water into a small saucepan and place on a low heat. When sugar has dissolved, bring syrup to boil and boil to soft ball stage, 115C (240F). In a large bowl, whisk egg whites until stiff. Gradually pour in sugar syrup, whisking all the time. Continue whisking until meringue is firm and cool. In a bowl, whip cream lightly and fold into meringue mixture with fruit purée.

Divide mixture between 6 ramekin dishes and freeze for 2-3 hours. Transfer to the refrigerator about 30 minutes before serving. Decorate with raspberries and mint.

Serves 6.

Note: For a special occasion, prepare small ramekin dishes by securing pieces of foil around them, to come above top of dish. Keep in place with freezer tape. Pour mixture into dishes to come over the top, so when foil removed, they look like risen soufflés.

1 large ripe pineapple with leaves
1-2 tablespoons kirsch
1 litre (32 fl oz/4 cups) vanilla ice cream
3 egg whites
185 g (6 oz/¾ cup) caster sugar
1 tablespoon caster sugar for sprinkling

Cut pineapple and leafy 'plume' in half lengthwise. Using a grapefruit knife, cut out flesh. Discard core, then cut flesh into chunks and put into a bowl. Sprinkle with kirsch, cover with plastic wrap and chill overnight with pineapple shells.

Put pineapple chunks back into shells and pack ice cream on top. Put in freezer for about 2 hours, until very firm. Meanwhile, preheat oven to 200C (400F/Gas 6). Just before serving, whisk egg whites in a bowl until stiff. Whisk in half the sugar, whisking for 1 minute more. Fold in remaining sugar.

Pile this meringue over ice cream, making sure it is completely covered. Make small peaks in meringue with a flat-bladed knife. Place pineapple shells on a baking sheet and sprinkle with the 1 tablespoon caster sugar. Bake in the oven for about 8 minutes, until meringue is browned. Serve immediately.

Serves 6.

Variation: Try making this dessert using a fruit sorbet instead of ice cream.

GOOSEBERRY ICE CREAM

750 g (1½ lb) gooseberries, thawed if frozen
125 g (4 oz/½ cup) caster sugar
3 egg yolks
1 small avocado
315 ml (10 fl oz/1¼ cups) whipping cream
gooseberries, leaves or borage flowers, to decorate, if
    desired

Put gooseberries into a saucepan with 2 tablespoons water and cook over a low heat until soft. Purée in a blender or food processor, then sieve to remove pips. Set aside to cool.

Put sugar into a saucepan with 2 tablespoons water, dissolve over medium heat, then boil syrup to thread stage, 110C (225F) on a sugar thermometer. In a bowl, beat egg yolks lightly, then pour syrup onto them and whisk until mixture is thick and mousse-like. Peel avocado, discard stone and mash flesh. Mix into gooseberry purée. Whip cream and fold into egg mixture with purée. Turn into rigid plastic container and freeze for 1-2 hours until beginning to be firm.

Remove from freezer and beat well. Freeze until firm. Transfer to refrigerator to soften for 30 minutes before serving. Serve in scoops in chilled glasses. Decorate each one with gooseberries, leaves or borage flowers.

Serves 4-6.

Note: Avocado gives this ice-cream a lovely texture. Its taste is not discernible.
    When cooking acidic fruits, such as gooseberries, do not use an aluminium pan. The fruit will taste metallic.

LYCHEE & PORT ICE CREAM

125 g (4 oz/½ cup) caster sugar
155 ml (5 fl oz/⅔ cup) ruby port
20 fresh lychees or 470 g (15 oz) can lychees
4 teaspoons fresh lime juice
315 ml (10 fl oz/1¼ cups) double (thick) cream
fresh or canned lychees and lime peel twists, to decorate

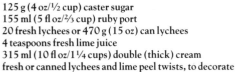
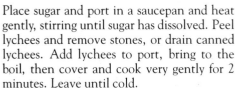

Place sugar and port in a saucepan and heat gently, stirring until sugar has dissolved. Peel lychees and remove stones, or drain canned lychees. Add lychees to port, bring to the boil, then cover and cook very gently for 2 minutes. Leave until cold.

Put port and lychees into a food processor fitted with a metal blade and process until smooth. Pour mixture into a sieve over a bowl and rub mixture through sieve using a wooden spoon. Stir in lime juice. Whip cream in a bowl until thick, add port mixture and fold in until evenly blended. Pour mixture into a plastic container, cover and freeze for 1-2 hours until mixture is almost frozen but still mushy.

Return mixture to processor and process until smooth and creamy. Return mixture to plastic container and freeze until firm. Scoop ice cream into serving dishes and decorate with lychees and lime peel.

Serves 6.

SAUCES &
ACCOMPANIMENTS

BLACKCURRANT SAUCE

250 g (8 oz) fresh or frozen blackcurrants, thawed if
   frozen
60 g (2 oz/¼ cup) caster sugar
2 tablespoons crème de cassis

Put blackcurrants into a saucepan with the
sugar and 125 ml (4 fl oz/½ cup) water, and
cook them over a medium heat until they are
tender.

Drain fruit, reserving juice. Push fruit
through a sieve with a little juice to make a
purée. Stir in cassis and enough of reserved
juice to give desired consistency. Serve cold.

Serves 4-6.

Note: Serve Blackcurrant Sauce with any of
the following recipes: Vanilla Bavarois (see
page 11), Coeurs à la Crème (see page 16),
Crêpe Ribbons (see page 34), Spotted Dick
(see page 49) or Cream Cheese Strudel (see
page 82).

MOUSSELINE SAUCE

1 egg, plus 1 extra yolk
45 g (1½ oz/8 teaspoons) caster sugar
2 tablespoons cream sherry

Put all ingredients into the top of a double
boiler or a bowl set over a saucepan of
simmering water.

Using a balloon whisk, whisk ingredients
until very thick and foamy. This will take at
least 10 minutes. Serve sauce at once.

Serves 4.

Note: Serve Mousseline Sauce with any of
the following recipes: Apple Charlotte (see
page 48), Pears in Wine (see page 52), Caramel Fruit Kebabs (see page 46) or Spotted
Dick (see page 49).

CRÈME À LA VANILLE

315 ml (10 fl oz/1¼ cups) creamy milk
1 vanilla pod
2 large egg yolks
1 tablespoon caster sugar
1 teaspoon cornflour or arrowroot

Put milk and vanilla pod into a saucepan. Bring almost to boiling point, then remove from heat, cover and leave to infuse for 5-10 minutes in the pan.

In a bowl, beat egg yolks, sugar and cornflour or arrowroot together. Pour the hot milk onto the mixture, stirring all the time and discarding the vanilla pod.

Return to rinsed-out pan and heat gently without boiling, stirring all the time, until sauce has thickened sufficiently to coat the back of the spoon. Strain into a jug and serve hot or cold.

Serves 4.

Note: Serve Crème à la Vanille with any of the following recipes: Bread & Butter Pudding (see page 18), Crêpe Ribbons (see page 34) or Spotted Dick (see page 49).

RASPBERRY SAUCE

250 g (8 oz) fresh or frozen raspberries
2 tablespoons lemon juice
60-90 g (2-3 oz/¼-⅓ cup) caster sugar
75 ml (2½ fl oz/⅓ cup) Framboise liqueur or water

Put all ingredients into a saucepan and bring slowly to boiling point.

Simmer for a few minutes, then either serve immediately, or rub through a nylon sieve (if you do not have a nylon one, use a wooden – not metal – spoon to rub fruit through a metal sieve, otherwise fruit will have a metallic taste). Serve the sauce cold.

Serves 4-6.

Note: Serve Raspberry Sauce with any of the following recipes: Cabinet Pudding (see page 13), Orange Roulade (see page 71), Crêpe Ribbons (see page 34), Rice & Fruit Mould (see page 20), Spotted Dick (see page 49) or Beignets (see page 80).

MINCEMEAT SAUCE

2 well-flavoured eating apples
2 small bananas
juice and grated peel of 1 lemon
185 g (6 oz) grapes
22 g (¾ oz/4½ teaspoons) butter
75 g (2¼ oz/⅓ cup) slivered almonds
30 g (1 oz/2 tablespoons) currants
30 g (1 oz/2 tablespoons) sultanas
rum or brandy, to taste

Peel, core and finely dice apples and bananas. Sprinkle with lemon juice.

Halve and seed grapes. Melt butter in a saucepan and fry almonds over medium heat until turning brown. Add prepared fruits with the lemon juice, grated lemon peel and currants and sultanas.

Stir over heat for a few minutes, then flavour with rum or brandy. Serve hot.

Serves 4-6.

Note: If the sauce is too tart, stir in a little brown sugar. Serve Mincemeat Sauce with any of the following recipes: Vanilla Bavarois (see page 11), Crêpe Ribbons (see page 34), Beignets (see page 80) or with scoops of vanilla ice cream.

DARK CHOCOLATE SAUCE

185 g (6 oz) plain (dark) chocolate
125 ml (4 fl oz/½ cup) strong black coffee or water
60 g (2 oz/¼ cup) caster sugar

Break chocolate into pieces and put in the top of a double boiler or a bowl set over a saucepan of simmering water. Add the coffee or water and sugar.

Stir over medium heat until the chocolate has melted and the sauce is smooth and creamy. Serve hot or cold.

Serves 4-6.

Note: Serve Dark Chocolate Sauce with any of the following recipes: Vanilla Bavarois (see page 11), Mixed Chocolate Terrine (see page 48), Hot Chocolate Soufflé (see page 50), Chocolate Ring Cake (see page 54), Chocolate Profiteroles (see page 87), or serve it hot with vanilla ice cream.

BITTER MOCHA SAUCE

90 g (3 oz) bitter plain (dark) chocolate
1 tablespoon dark, very strong, coarsely ground expresso coffee grounds
315 ml (10 fl oz/1¼ cups) whipping cream
7 g (¼ oz/1½ teaspoons) butter

Break chocolate into small pieces and place in the top of a double boiler or a bowl. Set aside. Put coffee and cream into a saucepan, bring to boil, then remove from heat and leave to infuse for 30 minutes.

Strain creamy coffee through a fine sieve onto the chocolate. Place over a pan of simmering water and stir until chocolate has melted.

Whisk in butter to make sauce glossy and serve at once.

Serves 6-8.

Note: Serve Bitter Mocha Sauce with any of the following recipes: Vanilla Bavarois (see page 11), Coffee Bombe (see page 86) or Mixed Chocolate Terrine (see page 62).

HOT LEMON SAUCE

juice and grated peel of 3 lemons
90 g (3 oz/⅓ cup) butter
90 g (3 oz/⅓ cup) caster sugar
1 rounded teaspoon cornflour

Put lemon juice and peel in a saucepan with butter and sugar. Stir over gentle heat until butter has melted and sugar dissolved.

Mix cornflour to a smooth paste with a little water and stir into the pan. Bring the sauce to the boil, stirring constantly.

Simmer for 1-2 minutes, stirring all the time. Keep warm until ready to serve.

Serves 4-6.

Note: Serve Hot Lemon Sauce with any of the following recipes: Crêpe Ribbons (see page 34), Lemon Belvoir Pudding (see page 47), Beignets (see page 80) or Austrian Curd Cheesecake (see page 21).

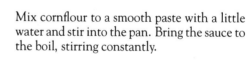

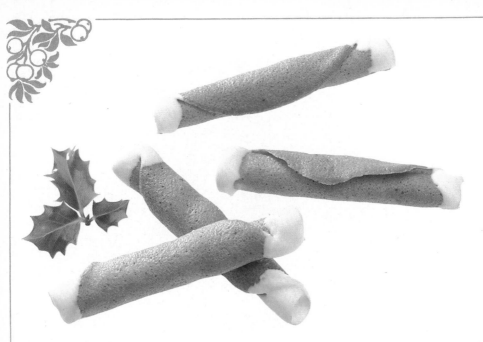

CHOCOLATE CIGARETTES

CRÈME DE MENTHE BISCUITS

2 egg whites
100 g (3½ oz/⅓ cup plus 3 teaspoons) caster sugar
52 g (1¾ oz/¼ cup plus 9 teaspoons) plain flour
2 teaspoons cocoa
60 g (2 oz/¼ cup) unsalted butter, melted
60 g (2 oz) white chocolate, melted

250 g (8 oz) plain (dark) chocolate
30 g (1 oz/6 teaspoons) butter
220 g (7 oz/2 cups) digestive biscuit crumbs
90 g (3 oz/¾ cup) plain cake crumbs
caster sugar for sprinkling

FILLING: 60 g (2 oz/¼ cup) unsalted butter
125 g (4 oz/¾ cup) icing sugar, sieved
2 teaspoons crème de menthe

Preheat oven to 200C (400F/Gas 6). Line 2 baking sheets with non-stick baking paper. Place egg whites in a bowl and whisk until stiff. Add caster sugar gradually, whisking well after each addition. Sift flour and cocoa over surface of mixture, add butter and fold in carefully until mixture is evenly blended.

Make filling first. Place butter in a bowl and beat with a wooden spoon until soft and smooth. Gradually beat in icing sugar and crème de menthe until light and fluffy.

Place 3 spoonfuls of mixture onto each baking sheet, well spaced apart. Spread each into a thin round. Bake, one sheet at a time, in the oven for 3-4 minutes, loosen each round with a palette knife, then return to the oven for 1 minute.

Break up chocolate and place in a bowl. Add butter and place over a saucepan of hand-hot water. Stir occasionally until melted. Add biscuit and cake crumbs and stir until evenly mixed and mixture forms a ball. Sprinkle a 25 cm (10 in) square of foil with caster sugar.

Take out one chocolate round at a time and quickly roll around a greased chopstick, or wooden spoon handle, to form a tube. Slip off and cool cigarette on a wire rack. Repeat with remaining rounds. Cook second tray of mixture, then repeat to make about 25 cigarettes. Dip both ends of each cigarette into melted chocolate. Leave to set on a paper-lined baking sheet. Store in an airtight container until required.

Roll out chocolate mixture on the foil to a 20 cm (8 in) square. Spread crème de menthe mixture evenly over chocolate square to within 1 cm (½ in) of edges. Roll up carefully into a neat roll using the foil to help. Wrap in foil and chill until firm. Cut into thin slices as and when required.

Makes 20 slices.

Makes 25.

TINY CHOCOLATE LOGS

3 eggs
45 g (1½ oz/8 teaspoons) caster sugar
30 g (1 oz/¼ cup) plain flour
3 teaspoons cocoa

FILLING AND DECORATION: 315 ml (10 fl oz/1¼ cups)
   double (thick) cream
125 g (4 oz) plain (dark) chocolate
marzipan toadstools

Preheat oven to 200C (400F/Gas 6). Line a 30 cm (12 in) baking tray (with edges) with non-stick baking paper. Place eggs and sugar in a bowl over a saucepan of simmering water and whisk until thick and pale.

Remove bowl from saucepan, continue whisking until mixture leaves a trail when whisk is lifted. Sift flour and cocoa onto surface of mixture and fold in carefully until mixture is evenly blended. Pour mixture onto baking tray and spread out carefully to edges. Bake in the oven for 8-10 minutes, or until firm to touch. Cool slightly, turn out and remove paper, then trim edges and cut in half lengthwise. Place 60 ml (2 fl oz/¼ cup) cream in a bowl with chocolate. Place over a pan of hot water; stir until melted. Whip remaining cream until almost thick.

When chocolate has cooled, fold it carefully into whipped cream. Using ⅓ chocolate cream, spread over each strip of sponge. Roll each into a firm roll from the long edge. Wrap in plastic wrap and chill until firm. Cut each roll into 6 lengths, spread each with remaining chocolate cream, mark cream into lines. Decorate with marzipan toadstools. Keep the rolls cool until ready to serve.

Makes 12.

BRANDY BUTTER

185 g (6 oz/¾ cup) unsalted butter
185 g (6 oz/¾ cup) caster sugar
90 ml (3 fl oz/⅓ cup) brandy

Put butter in a bowl or food processor fitted with a metal blade. Beat or process butter until white and creamy. Add sugar and beat or process until light and fluffy.

Add brandy, a drop at a time, beating continuously until enough has been added to well-flavour the butter. Take care the mixture does not curdle through overbeating.

Pile butter into a glass dish and serve with a spoon, or, if preferred, spread the mixture about 1 cm (½ in) thick over a flat dish and leave to set hard. Using a fancy cutter, cut Brandy Butter into shapes and arrange in a serving dish.

Serves 8.

INDEX